Fiona Parashar is founder of Leadership Coaching Ltd, an executive coaching company whose clients include Donna Karan Retail UK Ltd, Universal Studios Networks UK Ltd, Carlton Screen Advertising, Sky and Associated Newspapers. She specializes in coaching senior executives through transitionary periods, typically promotions, restructures, mergers or new roles, but also mid-life transitions in the context of work.

Work–life balance, is at the heart of her work for herself, her associates and her clients. Her coaching style is powerful yet soothing, combining her business experience with her academic background in Psychology and Psychotherapy.

Fiona spent twelve years in advertising and media, which saw her at top international agencies, Ogilvy, Lintas and McCann Erickson. She latterly jointly ran a top media company, Universal McCann, whose clients included Nestle, Sky, Loreal, Coca Cola, before leaving to set up Leadership Coaching.

Fiona's academic qualifications include Human Psychology (BSc Hons) and Psychotherapy (DipTHP). She is also a Master Practitioner of Neuro Lingusitic Programming and accredited to administer and process psychometric testing (MBTI, FIRO-B and Emergenetics). She is a member of the International Coaching Federation.

She lives in North London with her husband and two children.

For Paul, Millie and Arthur

The Balancing Act

Work–life solutions
for busy people

FIONA PARASHAR

SIMON & SCHUSTER

LONDON • NEW YORK • SYDNEY • TOKYO • SINGAPORE • TORONTO • DUBLIN

First published in Great Britain by Simon & Schuster UK Ltd, 2003
A Viacom company

1 3 5 7 9 10 8 6 4 2

Simon & Schuster UK Ltd
Africa House
64–78 Kingsway
London WC2B 6AH

www.simonsays.co.uk

Simon & Schuster Australia
Sydney

A CIP catalogue record for this book is available
from the British Library

ISBN 0-7432-3112-0

Typeset in Plantin Light
by Palimpsest Book Production Limited,
Polmont, Stirlingshire
Printed and bound in Great Britain by
The Bath Press, Bath

Acknowledgements

The joy in writing this book has been immense as it has unfolded. It has untapped in me a part that has balanced me more deeply than had I not written it, and for that I will be ever grateful to my husband, Paul, for giving me the space, love and support to grow in this way.

Thank you also to my children, who have been amazing teachers already to me, and taught me many of the lessons I share in this book, especially to do with health and wellbeing.

I would also like to thank the rest of my family and Paul's for their support, especially the times when they so wonderfully spoiled our children whilst I was writing, researching, or attending a course.

Also a huge thanks to our nanny, Sophie, whose smiling consistency and flexibility has kept our family balanced through the roller coaster of setting up businesses and book writing, new schools and constantly changing timetables.

A special thank you must go to Jackee Holder, my writing coach, who steered the book in a more personal way.

Jean Pierre le Blanc who has been my spiritual/health/wellbeing teacher/coach. I am more balanced and richer because of him.

Rachel Pryor who successfully coached me through the transition of setting up my business and its first stellar year with balance kept firmly at the top of the agenda.

I also wish to thank the people who so willingly gave up their time for in-depth interviews on work–life balance and so graciously shared their ideas and thinking.

Acknowledgements

Jayne Buxton from Flametree (Work–life Balance Solutions), Joanne Forster, (campaigner on work–life balance), Sarah Jackson (Parents at Work) Lynne Franks (author and founder of Seedfusion, president of Globalfusion),

Andrew Samuels (Jungian analyst and Professor of Analytical Psychology, Essex University). Christine Walker (President of Work–life Balance in Advertising), Debbie Klein (planner and author of Research on Balance Issues for Women), Kirsten Furber (Discovery Networks, instigator of government funded Work–life Balance Initiative) and Monty Alexander (Semiotic Solutions).

I also am extremely grateful for the learning I have received from my clients who are living proof of the work–life issues that we are all facing, especially to those who have so unhesitatingly allowed me to use their case studies in the book to support my ideas.

To my researchers, Kelly Taylor and Alice Sherman, who so painstakingly researched all of my requests, however bizarre or difficult they were.

Tessa Allingham who was a superb editor and honest friend throughout every stage of the manuscript.

My Associates, Sue Hartley, Imogen Brown, Sandra Visser and Chris Loe, for their backing, patience and enthusiasm.

Cathy Fischgrund and Michael Alcock, my agents, who believed in the idea straight away and made it all happen, effortlessly.

At Simon and Schuster, I'd like to thank Helen Gummer for believing in the book and being so committed, and Cassie Campbell for being an excellent project manager, a steady and supportive voice, always there. And to Kathy Gale for her enthusiasm and backing.

Contents

Introduction

We all want more balance. We are worn down and worn out, crazed from the spinning madness that has become normality. It takes little more than a glance around us to see exhaustion, stress and frustration etched on our faces. As extraordinary demands are placed on us in the workplace and we are expected to work in ways that are both unfamiliar and not of our choosing, more and more of us are experiencing a sense of spinning out of kilter, of life controlling us rather than the other way round.

We're out of whack, and not only want but also need to get things back on track. The plaintive cries of disgruntled workers are heard bouncing off the walls in industry as talent drains out of corporations and goes in search of better work–life balance.

Yet it doesn't have to be that way. Our lives do not have to be dominated by exhaustion, stress and frustration. We can achieve a work–life balance that's right for us by facing up to and, where necessary, altering our relationship with work. The key to achieving this balance is in working in harmony with our work, rather than against it, working in harmony with time, rather than fighting it, and working in harmony with life rather than just bobbing through it like a cork in tumultuous waters. If we feel we are in a happy, meaningful, fulfilling relationship with our work, we are better able to deal with our life as a whole.

In researching and writing this book, I sought answers to the question of how best we can achieve more balance in our lives. For I had become mystified as to why so many people feel out of balance, and why this feeling is now reaching such a peak as more and more exhausted, frustrated, stressed people cry out for help – or just give up.

Don't give up.

Don't give in.

The mystery has been solved for I am a mystery-solver. At least, that is how I like to think of myself, but when I set out on solving the mystery of missing work–life balance, little did I know the amazing journey I would take.

I embarked on this extraordinary task some years ago when faced with a sense of dizzy craziness at the way I and others were living our lives. All around me I could hear and see people searching for balance but somehow feeling powerless to do anything. It was a desire to help solve this mystery that led me to write this book. Why are so many of us so out of balance, I wondered? Why is it so widespread, why now? Could elements of my own experience be translated to other people's situations? What are the common characteristics of a life that's in balance, and one that's not? What causes both? I felt that if I was able to answer these questions I would be able to solve the mystery.

In searching for the answers I have learned more than I could ever have imagined, and I continue to learn. I have read myriad scientific papers and books, I have interviewed scores of people, I have looked both into and outside the business world for clues. My journey has taken me to strange and diverse sources, from physicists to poets, from tightrope walkers to CEOs, from professors to psychic healers, from doctors to teachers, and bankers to secretaries. It has been fascinating to see the mystery unfold and develop. It has turned out to be much more complex a mystery than I ever expected, yet strangely simple once I had made the first few connections. In the chapters that follow I bring the clues together but I invite you to piece them together yourself in order to solve the mystery of your own work–life balance. I present the information I have discovered and it's up to you to take that information and use the ideas, theories and exercises in a way that makes sense to *you*.

I have been sceptical, stunned, excited and inspired by this mystery. In the beginning, I had no idea where my questioning would lead. Frankly, I thought work–life balance was just a case of moving to a three-day week. Now I see that the mystery can be solved on many different levels.

I found that work should be an energizer, not a drainer; that balance goes on inside the head; that it is powerfully linked to work, diet, health, intuition and relationships, and that it's about being brave and taking new steps. It's also about being vulnerable and accepting and honouring the different sides to our personality. It's about growth and development.

I found that people are transformed once they solve the mystery for themselves. Finding a good work–life balance is a life-changing and life-enhancing experience. Magic happens. Metaphoric rabbits pop out of hats, transformations take place, spectacular and amazing feats are performed.

I found also that the mystery is never completely solved. The case is never closed. It's like finding out who the murderer is but not knowing why they did it. So we solve the mystery on one level, but on another our curiosity keeps the case open.

I will always be solving this mystery of balance. It's a story that continues throughout our lives. But balance is possible and obtainable, more easily than we perhaps thought. We have lost our way, but it need only be a temporary loss of direction. We can get back on track. Reading this book and following the exercises will get your life back in balance.

How this book works

This book looks first at *why* we feel out of balance, then *what* we can do about it, and finally *how*, by following the strategies and exercises outlined here, we can achieve more balance in our lives. Here's a brief synopsis of what's in store in the pages that follow.

Chapters 1, 2 and 3 explore the reasons we are out of balance. In essence, it's because we have gone too far in one direction, either at work, in society or individually, and are now striving to regain our equilibrium on many different levels. In other words, we are experiencing a counterbalance against a world that has become too busy, too material, too harsh. And we are, I believe, experiencing this both collectively as a society, and individually, since the rise of the feminine spirit has counterbalanced masculine energy, leaving us feeling the need for more than materialism and productivity, and questioning not only who we are but also what we should be doing with our lives. Once we understand the 'why' we can start to make changes. Once we have done that, then we can move on to the 'what'.

What we can do about this imbalance is covered in Chapters 4 and 5. In Chapter 4, I argue that there are no valid *reasons* for imbalance – they're just *excuses* masquerading as reasons. And the inability to get more balance in our lives stems not from these surface-level excuses but from the fear that lies underneath them. Only once we have dug deep and faced our fear, are we ready to move on to getting more balance in our lives. In Chapter 5, I explore the importance of discovering what I call our Personal Band of Balance (PBB), that unique place within us where we feel balanced. Amazingly, this band of balance is easily achieved and is inextricably linked to our relationship with work. This is not a book that advocates the way to better work–life balance is necessarily by downshifting or working part time. All my research indicates that getting work 'right', i.e. being more effective and enjoying work, is a vital component to getting more balance in our lives.

And finally, in Chapters 6 to 8, I look at how to achieve balance by following the three 'macro strategies'. These are choosing health, using our intuition, and heightening our own self-awareness. They're small words but huge topics, for they are the building blocks of a life in balance.

For those who like practical, easy-to-follow steps, I've devised a mini programme at the end of each chapter which encourages interaction with the concepts discussed. These exercises do make a difference, and are underpinned with suggestions for 'rituals' to include in your daily routine. These rituals instil new and more productive behaviours, which help make the transition from thought to action. I am a big fan of action. Talking about things and not doing them can be a real stressor. If you create action, on the other hand, the changes will follow.

In the final chapter I give a 7-day plan, which is designed to kickstart the reprogramming of the brain, if you like, to accept some new, more effective and more balanced ways of working, both in your professional and home life.

My mystery

A life in balance is one in which opportunity and choice bloom. A life out of balance is one in which opportunities seem scarce. Believe me: I have firsthand experience of both existences, as well as having witnessed them countless times in the clients I coach. One of the most important things to remember is that you don't necessarily have to downshift or start working part time to achieve a successful work–life balance. Provided you are prepared to make some key behavioural changes, you can find a balance that's right for you in your current situation. I have exchanged a stressed, spinning, tiring life for an energizing, fulfilling, balanced one. Does it mean I have less power, status or money? No.

Do I have more time with my family and friends? Do I enjoy my life more, do I feel in control? Yes.

Do I believe that it is possible for everyone to achieve this? I do.

Let me relate my own story. I knew something was wrong about Christmas time. I felt sick. What was I doing? I had two small babies and was working full time as joint managing director of a multi-million pound media company. I had just spent the Christmas holidays with my family and I realized during those heady, holiday days exactly what I was missing. I was missing out on my own babies' babyhood and their growth. It suddenly made no sense to me. It was a mystery.

Why had I given birth to two beautiful babies and then decided to leave them for somebody else to look after Monday to Friday? What had seemed fine previously suddenly seemed not at all fine.

The importance of choice

I had to get to the bottom of it. I soon realized that part of the problem was that *I thought I had no choice*. It was a case of *'I have to earn that money and do that job because that's what I do.'* I hadn't even thought to question it.

Choice. It's a humble yet wonderful word and this is where the search for balance starts and ends. It is the biggest clue to this mystery of our missing balance. We have lost sight of the fact that *we do have choices*. Indeed, living life the way many now do, stressed and always busy, is a choice. These are choices we've made and are making every day, except we don't think of them as such. We may not be making these choices consciously but, at some level, we have chosen to run our lives in such a way that we are becoming tired and stressed.

'I haven't chosen it, I have no choice in this, it has just happened to me. Why would I choose to make myself that distant from my family?' This is the defence I often hear because we do not recognize that we have made a choice. We simply slip into patterns of behaviour that we deem to be inevitable. But they are not inevitable. We do have choice.

From unconscious incompetence to conscious incompetence

One of the first things I did was to start making the shift from *unconscious incompetence* to *conscious incompetence*, i.e. I realized I didn't feel happy with the situation and that something was wrong. This is my favourite model. I don't know who invented it, but it's used frequently in coaching and training sessions to describe our way of learning. It sums up neatly what happens during the process of coaching as we move from blissful (or should I say unblissful) ignorance through a newfound crystalization of what's going wrong, into developing new and more effective behaviours and finally integrating them into our personality so that they become second nature.

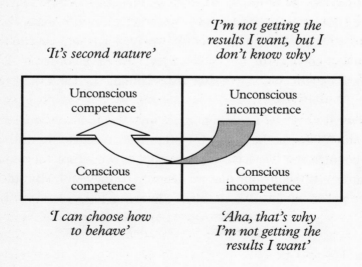

'It's second nature'   *'I'm not getting the results I want, but I don't know why'*

| Unconscious competence | Unconscious incompetence |
| Conscious competence | Conscious incompetence |

'I can choose how to behave'   *'Aha, that's why I'm not getting the results I want'*

The learning cycle

In writing this book, I aim to help you understand where you're going 'wrong', to enable you to learn new, more effective and balanced ways of living and working, and to make them an effortless part of your life.

For me, my state of *unconscious incompetence* was caused by the fact that I hadn't questioned or thought about what I was doing and whether my lifestyle really matched my true values in my new role as a mother. I had continued with business as usual. When I received my Christmas wake-up call I became aware of what it was that I wasn't doing. Once I became aware, I was able to make a choice. Did I want to continue unquestioning or did I want to question? I'd shifted into a state of *conscious incompetence* and that, as I tell all my clients, is progress indeed: at least once we know what it is we're doing 'wrong' or incompetently, we can start to make some conscious choices about it.

I decided to question. I pieced all the clues together. Why did I go to work? What did I want from work? What did work give me that being at home with my children couldn't? What did being with my children give me that work couldn't? What benefit was I reaping from feeling so stressed and stretched? What did I get from being so frenetic, so busy? What would alleviate my guilt? What did I actually want from work and life?

I wanted to be with my children and I wanted to work. But I wanted my work to be so incredibly enjoyable and stimulating and true to me that when I was away from my babies it would never cause me to wish I was back with them. It would be so invigorating and nourishing in its own right that I would be happy to leave them secure in the knowledge that I would have enough time with both parts of my life that I would never feel guilty about the other one.

So, mystery solved. Or was it more a case of just opened?

In a sense, it was both. Solved in that I had found the cause of my feelings of imbalance. Opened in that it was a mystery how I was going to go from guilt to glory, from stressed to serene. Was this Utopia I hankered after just a dream or was it possible? Yes, it was possible, yes it is, and here I am, some years on from that point having achieved a work–life balance that's right for me. It feels like another life, I feel liberated, I feel rich. Indeed, I *am* liberated and I *am* rich, in the fullest sense of the word, in relationships, opportunities and in my own wellbeing.

The person that I used to be was too busy to be a good wife or mum, too busy to be a good friend. She would regularly forget birthdays and nice gestures, was often curt on the telephone and impatient when a train was scheduled to arrive in three minutes rather than one. She couldn't wait with someone for a lift to arrive, she'd just say goodbye and leave in the hope of clawing back another 30 seconds. She was sometimes even too busy to go to the bathroom! She drank eight or so coffees a day and raced through life at a relentless, dizzying speed. She had no time to notice anything really, except the world spinning by, crazed in a fight against time. That person has now gone, thank goodness. She has been replaced by someone calmer and less stressed, for whom the word 'busy' has positive and meaningful connotations and stress is something to be avoided wherever possible, or at least dealt with proactively.

I do not want negative stress. We all know that some stress can be healthy, but that exhausting, debilitating, frenetic stress is something I seek to keep out of my life now. I want focus, I want power, I want influence and productivity, but I want it without negative stress. Is that possible all the time?

To be honest, no. Is it possible most of the time? Yes. Welcome new person, new life.

Through the process of discovering my new personality and my new life, I realized that it was a *choice*. I had been *choosing* the former way to live, and now I have *chosen* another. I had found the key to unlocking the mystery of work–life balance, the biggest clue: *how we live our days is our choice*.

My mystery solved . . . on one level

The other clues fell into place after that. Having reached the state of *conscious incompetence*, I had to decide what I wanted to do to move to the next stage of *conscious competence*. I wanted to run my own business – doing what? Psychology, coaching and writing – where? Working from home – how often? Three days a week – with whom? Business people who wanted to achieve their full potential, people who wanted to gain better work–life balance. In order to achieve my goals, I found myself a coach who helped pull all the clues out of me and enabled me to solve my mystery.

Of course, this was just the start, but having dealt with the key issues, the complex matters of setting up a business and a new way of life fell into place stunningly easily. It was a seamless and liberating transition. Now, several years on, I feel I have reached a state of *unconscious competence*, in which I instinctively know when things are going wrong and I'm able to get myself back in balance far more quickly. I have become more skilled at judging what's needed to keep my own life in equipoise, I balance and counterbalance all the time. It has become second nature to me.

The secret of work–life balance

It's unique

It became clear very early on in my research that what constitutes balance varies hugely from person to person. It would be pointless to impose any textbook definition, since each individual's balance and the way each person should work to achieve that balance is unique. One of the most intriguing discoveries I have made has been that of the Personal Band of Balance (PBB), as I've chosen to call it. It's that place, hidden and un-named until now, we all have inside us, which, when we operate within it, either in a work or home situation, ensures we feel perfectly in balance.

It's an inner balance

This band of balance turns out to be in our heads. We won't find our work–life balance at home, in the office, by flexi-working or by taking longer holidays. We'll find it in our heads. Balance has almost nothing to do with how much we do or don't work. It astounded me to realize this, since I assumed that working fewer hours was the obvious answer to the problem. There's no doubt that it can *help*, but there isn't the direct correlation I had anticipated. During my research, I interviewed people who work only one day a week and yet feel out of balance, as well as others who work a five-day week or more and feel totally in balance. The key is *choice* and *control*. If a person feels it's their choice and if they feel in control, then bring on the hours.

I myself experienced this when I first set up my own business. I moved from working a five-day week to working a three-day week, and for a time I still felt out of balance. Why? Because I was a whirligig of ecstasy and manic energy so, even though I was working fewer hours and thoroughly enjoying the adrenalin-induced buzz it created inside me, I was more out of balance because there was no calm inside my head. It was a great lesson. There is no magic formula correlating the number of days worked to balance. The truth is that the only thing we can completely control and make genuine choices about is . . . ourselves. If we can control ourselves and choose our responses, then we can make progress. It's inside. Not outside.

What I also discovered during my research – and through coaching – is just how much people are aware of and understand the concept of a PBB. Every person I interviewed for this book, and every person I have coached *knows* what it feels like to be balanced, knows what it looks like, sounds like and feels like to be in balance. What's more, they know what throws them in and out of balance and, even if they don't know how to go about achieving it, they know *what it takes* to get back into balance. Seems implausible? It's not. This book gives all the tools and techniques necessary to access your own PBB.

It's dynamic

It also became clear that *work–life balance is not static*. It changes. Our idea of what constitutes a balanced life does not necessarily remain the same from week to week. It might, but life changes daily. Our moods, energy, priorities, interests, workloads and life events can all alter. Rarely can we predict with precision what a day will throw at us. So yesterday's balance strategies may have to be readjusted to deal with the problems of today.

Balance is dynamic. Accepting this and working with it is liberating. We need to keep looking at it and adjusting the 'weights' on our life scales accordingly. However, rather than using great big weights that send the metaphoric scales crashing from side to side, it is much more effective to adjust the scales using small weights that elicit only tiny movements. This subject is covered in more detail in Chapter 5.

So, read on now, to learn about what has knocked us out of balance and what we can do to put things right. If you prefer, you can go straight to the chapter that most interests you, but you are likely to have a better understanding of the context if you read the preceding chapters first.

WHY . . .

are we out of balance?

What's happening in
the workplace

I

Out of Balance

What's going on at work?

When I coach, I listen.

I listen with my ears to the twists in tonality, the quickening of my client's speech, the outpouring at speed, or the animated excitement of something that interests them. I also listen with my eyes, noticing body movements, where their eyes are looking, the hand gestures, the slumping of the body.

I listen with my body, wondering why I am experiencing certain sensations when some words are spoken. I hear my body tell me when someone is telling me – and himself or herself – a lie. I sense when someone is in pain, and when an idea is bursting forth. Most of all, I listen with my heart. My heart hears the options that are hiding there but aching to get out, it hears the potential in everybody, the creativity and spirit.

And, of course, I listen quietly, withholding judgment. I hear thoughts that have never been spoken before and, as they are spoken, they become crystallized. For thoughts are formed by our language and our language forms our thought. In hearing these thoughts spoken aloud I know that people want more, I know they want something different, I know they want to re-connect with the important things in their lives. I know people are bewildered by how far off course they seem to have drifted, without even noticing. I know that people want change, but that they don't know how to achieve it.

And I know I can help.

I have spent many years in industry wrestling with the problem of work–life balance, both as a working mum myself, and as a manager of over 100 members of staff. Now, in my role as an outside consultant and executive coach specializing in work–life balance, I approach the problem from a more objective perspective. What has become absolutely fascinating to me, is that in helping people gain better work–life balance I have heard a consistent theme: people only feel truly balanced if things are going well at work. If they feel in control at work, if they feel they are making a meaningful contribution, if they feel good at the end of the day, then other things fall into place. If I am coaching people who say they want more time with their families, friends or hobbies, I insist on them being specific about how much more time.

Now here is the surprise . . . the extra they are hankering after is often not very much. In many cases just a few hours more a week would do the trick. In a 60-hour week, and given some help and focus, it is actually very easy to find 4–5 extra hours.

When I delve further, it always comes back to the same thing. If they can get work 'right', the rest will fall into place. They won't go home feeling angry, guilty, distracted. If they feel in control, they can make positive, resourceful decisions about the important aspects of work and life. So it is essential to understand what is going on at work, and how to make it 'right'.

I have been listening to the cries for more balance for many years, but recently my ears feel fit to burst as I hear more and more cries for help. *'I want more balance, I'm knackered, I'm exhausted, I'm bored. I want a life.'* It sounds so desperate, but people somehow feel unable to make the changes that will achieve balance. *'I don't know what I want, I have no passions, no dreams, nothing I'm particularly good at,'* is the constant refrain.

'You're right,' I agree, for passionate dreams and excellence rarely breed on arid land. A tired, bored or stressed-out person has fewer ideas or concepts of choice than one that isn't. Our repertoire of options expands when we have positive emotions coursing through our body. This has been proven many times by psychologists. The American Psychological Association has been working with psychologist Barbara Fredrickson to prove the positive impact of positive emotions on health and wellbeing. When we are stressed or harbouring toxic emotions such as anger, sadness or fear, we become anxious and stressed and our repertoire of options closes down. We become myopic, tunnel-visioned, convinced that the way we are working is the only way things can be done, that the workload is just something we have to cope with, that the meetings have to be at that time, and conducted in that way.

Forget it. There are myriad choices as to how we handle our lives, day by day. Positive emotions such as interest, joy and contentment broaden our repertoire of choices (or our thought to action repertoire, as the psychologists call it). Fredrickson calls it the 'Broaden and Build' model of positive emotions. They broaden our outlook and they help build our physical and mental resources. So get interested, get joyful, for the more we can get these emotions in our lives, the more they negate the limiting power of the negative emotions. By proactively choosing positive emotions we increase our options. We begin to see we have choices of how we want each day to unfold. Then we can change our whole lives. Easily. A day at a time.

Scorn, snorts of derision, cynical looks, quizzical raising of the eyebrows, arm-crossing – these are the typical reactions when I tell clients this.

'It's all right for you,' they say.

'Yes!' I agree, *'but that's because I've made it all right for me. And you can make it all right for you too.'*

'But most people don't have my boss/my workload/my responsibilities/my pressures/my time shortage,' they counter.

'Oh yes they do.'

We are each of us unique in our personality and our situation but we are at one with millions of other people when it comes to the central themes of tiredness, stress, frustration, lack of energy and lack of balance. We are at one, when we point the finger at bosses, workloads, responsibilities and pressures; in fact when we point the finger at anything 'out there'. We are at one, and we are all wrong. For when we do that, we lose our power. The changes we desire will not come from 'out there'. We'll wait an eternity for that and it'll be an unbalanced eternity at that. The rebalancing changes must come from us. As we change, others will respond. We must be the change we want to have in our lives.

It goes without saying that not everyone feels like this. I have plenty of clients who are energized, purposeful and highly motivated. This book is not for them. It's for the many, many people who want to find more balance between work and life, who experience a huge tension between the two parts of their life. There should be no tension, just a relationship.

That is our goal. That is the journey we are embarking on, one that will leave us able to say, honestly, *'work creates pleasure and balance in my life'*. My life is balanced by fulfilling work. Their relationship is interdependent and positive. At best they can be one and the same.

Corporate trends

I have been listening to the corporate world and I have heard what is going on: the mergers and acquisitions, the relentless speed of change, the service culture, the price wars, the drive for shareholder value.

'Help, I'm drowning. Help, I'm on a treadmill. Help, I'm on a merry-go-round, I'm a spinning top. Save me, slow me down, help me off. Stop me spinning. I feel sick.'

This spinning madness has become the norm in the corporate world in recent years. And I hope that this book will help make the treadmills, merry-go-rounds, spinning tops and sense of drowning things of the past. We are not designed for dizziness. It makes us feel queasy and unbalanced.

Time pressures

But why are so many people feeling so out of balance? What has been going on in the workplace to create this feeling? This was a crucial part of the mystery, so I went into organizations and I asked and listened, and this is what I heard.

'I have no time. Nobody has any time.'

Well, that is a mystery in itself. How can nobody feel like they have any time? People are working longer hours than ever before, so the working day is actually longer than it has ever been. Therefore, surely, people actually have *more* time. When you take into account the timesaving technological advances in the workplace, this was a strange phenomenon indeed.

Employees today feel as if they do not have enough time. *'To do what?'* I ask. *'To think,'* they answer. Fire fighting and scurrying has replaced ideas, front feet and creativity, forcing the working life to become a life of deadlines. Deadline culture seems to have taken hold, nailing people so firmly to the line that is dead that they cannot see the life that is alive. The deadline becomes the sole focus, shutting out friends, family and politeness. Shutting out humanity. Shutting out choice. The deadline must be met. It's a race against time. Our perspective goes. A myopic viewpoint takes hold, as time becomes our enemy rather than our friend.

What, I wondered, could be causing this obsession with deadlines and such loss of perspective? I analyzed some corporate trends and I believe that there are three main factors behind this acrimonious and tense relationship with time that is knocking us out of balance. The first is caused by the *service culture* that now epitomizes many industries. The client is always right. Serve and obey the client, the customer. The mantra is to differentiate by service because product differentiation is so tough to achieve these days. And as departments within companies or schools or hospitals or governments become more specialized, accountable and self-funding, the internal customer seems to have become even more tricky to deal with than the external one.

The second is the *consolidation* through globalization and mergers and acquisitions. Everyone, it seems, is merging or being taken over or taking over or making strategic allegiances. Change in the workplace is constant and it's happening at a dizzying speed.

The third is the *knowledge revolution*, as management gurus such as Peter Drucker, Tom Peters and Charles Handy refer to it. They talk of us becoming a knowledge-based society where the role of an organization is to put knowledge to work. Knowledge is the currency by which we trade. It has replaced manual labour. Knowledge is now the key to personal and economic success. This has caused there to be greater emphasis on communication. And it's causing a lot of pain and problems in organizations.

My theory is that it is these three factors that are causing the malaise I constantly see in my role as a coach. Each leads directly to a sensation of imbalance. The service culture has led to a sense of *spinning*, the consolidation to *deadening*, and the knowledge revolution to *communication crises*. So let's have a look at each in turn.

The service culture and spinning

What do I mean by spinning? Most of us instinctively know. It's the constant dizzy agitation of someone out of control. It is how many of us get through the day. We spin our way through it. It is often called fire fighting, dealing with crises, or lurching from one situation to another with no sense of purposefulness or proactivity. The to-do list gets longer and longer, and the small dents we make in it just serve to taunt us in our ineffectiveness, which just makes us spin even more.

The sensation of spinning in organizations is highly infectious and within it there is a constant theme. No matter how successful they are, when people lose their sense of balance, it is down to one thing: they temporarily lose their resourcefulness, their power to problem-solve, to see things clearly, to keep a sense of perspective. They become a buffeted, spinning-top knocked about in the maelstrom of their environment and the people in it – in other words, by life.

In psychological terms, this is known as having an *external locus of control* – i.e. you perceive that control is outside your remit. *'It's nothing to do with me, it's not my fault, it's just happening to me, I can't do anything about it,'* we say to ourselves and to others. Once we sense that control is located outside our body, our ability to respond creatively to situations shuts down. Study after study has shown that people with an external locus of control are more likely to be anxious, stressed, unresourceful, less successful and less confident. They also have less sense of wellbeing and, ultimately, are prone to be ill.

So what's the key to changing this? Getting the locus of control back inside the body and making it an *internal* locus of control. When this happens, we believe we can effect change. This is a vital part of the process of regaining balance, and a subject we will revisit regularly throughout this book.

Buffeting our way to balance

The perceived supremacy of clients or customers and the emphasis on service exacerbates this situation because the message we receive is that the power is outside us, that it resides with the client. It encourages us to be buffeted. No more. We deliver far more for our clients if we stay in control. We must buffet with calm confidence. Psychological studies have shown that people with an internal locus of control have healthier, happier lifestyles. They are more successful, more confident, and have a better sense of wellbeing. This is what we all are after. And, ironically, it's what our clients want of us.

This idea is the central theme to successful living. It's the difference that unites purposeful workers and successful employees and is at the heart of every single personal development programme. Being in control of our own destiny, as it is often called, and not being a victim. We decide what we want and we organize ourselves, adapt our behaviour and change our environment in order to achieve it. Sure, things stand in our way in this process, but that's when we most need our sense of control to be inside rather than outside us. That's when we can calmly buffet things away, rather than be buffeted ourselves.

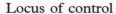

Locus of control

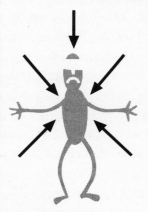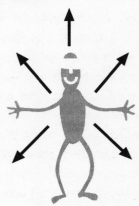

External
Locus of control
(things happen *to* me)

More likely to be
• anxious
• stressed
• less confident
• ill

Internal
Locus of control
(*I* can make things happen)

More likely to be
• confident
• successful
• healthy
• have a sense of wellbeing

So how do we internalize our locus of control, and take the power within? Well, that's what I hope this book will help you achieve through the exercises and techniques in each chapter, but the first step is to recognize its existence, and then locate it. Is it inside or outside of you? If it's outside, this book will provide plenty of opportunities to get it back inside. I work with the concept daily and I still cannot keep it inside me 100 per cent of the time. There are times when I feel completely self-pitying and buffeted by life's events, but I have increased, and keep on increasing, the amount of time it is inside me. Ask yourself what your ratio is and what you would like it to be. Often, people feel it is 40:60 with the external locus of control having the advantage. Internalizing control and flipping that balance to 60:40 has a tremendous impact. It stops the spinning.

In my experience, the spinners often really enjoy their work, but they are at the mercy of it. They are excited, enthused and wrapped up in life at the office. They lose their sense of balance because they are out of control. They do not spend enough time away from the office, a situation which they frequently lament, yet they believe there is no choice. The work must be done in this way. The world of work dictates how they live their lives. And because work is meaningful to them, albeit stressful, they mistakenly believe this is the only way. Their immersion causes them to lose perspective, they believe that *this is how it must be*. But that is just allowing the locus of control to sit outside of us. We need to internalize it. We should call the shots. Just keep increasing the internalizing, the taking the power inside . . . as much as you can and as often as you can. Believe you can take charge and make a difference, because you can.

Consolidation and deadening

Deadening. What a terrible word. Is some awful virus spreading through the western workplace that is slowly killing people off? With stress, absenteeism and staff churn (people leaving) at an all-time high, people are clearly suffering from something. What is deadening them?

The root of the problem lies in the fact that many people are not doing what they want to be doing. Most people are shoe-horned into roles that do not fit their strengths. If they're good at something they get promoted on the strength of that, and are then often thrown into a world of different skills that they neither enjoy nor possess. The constant change, mergers and acquisitions, and the integration of new people, new bosses and new cultures is also wearing people down. Internal politicking has taken on a whole new guise. It is the guise of fear, of unproductive running around, endless internal documents, inward competitiveness and a defensive stance. To what end?

Leaders need to be careful of the power they wield, because when they ask for something the whole place can go crazy. Arses get kicked, people panic, we can smell the fear. One of my roles as a coach is to help leaders see the ramifications of their actions. One manager, who had a very aggressive, mercurial style, which involved publicly berating his staff, wonders why, a year on – even though he no longer behaves in this way – people seem fearful of him and won't speak up with ideas or initiatives. *'Humans have long memories, and we scare easily,'* I remind him. *'Beware the power.'*

Another leader I coach related a story about how he had once casually told staff he'd be in the office on a Saturday. When he arrived, he found most of the company had turned up and that some had been in since 5 am. He said it made him realize the power of a throwaway remark. Beware the power. People often see roles, not humans. It's sad, but true.

People will always look upwards for direction, and if that upwards is constantly changing it is confusing and can cause people to become disconnected from the reason they turn up to work every day. Then it really is an awful virus, and it does slowly kill people off mentally. Unconnected to the meaning of their work, to their new role, or their new goals, the energy ebbs away, until the shell of a human tips up at work each day and emptily carries out its task. The rich dynamism of a challenging and engaged worker suddenly seems a rare thing.

I coach now in many organizations where people are consistently under performing, usually by one third to a half. Where is all that energy going? Is it channelled into social life outside the office? No. These people report flopping on the sofa at home. The energy has been quelled, deadened, dampened. When things are going well at work, when we feel in balance, doing what we enjoy, we seem effortlessly to achieve so much more in life. We feel as though we're sailing easily through life, full of beans and energy. As one client put it: *'When things go well at work, everything in my life runs smoothly. When work is bad, it's only then that I hanker after time with my family and feel that my work–life balance is out of whack.'* Her request to me was for help on getting work right. If she could achieve this, the rest would fall into place. This, I think, neatly sums up the issue. We spend so much time at work, and it plays such a pivotal role in our self-esteem and our relationship with our friends, family and life, that we need to get it right to feel truly balanced. If we feel a sense of deadened energy at work, it will spill over into our home life.

What has deadened us? It's a question of wrong roles and lost connections with too much meaningless work, rather than too much work per se. Most people are energized by a challenging workload, even a heavy one as long as it is meaningful to them. People aren't shirkers by nature if they're engaged. The continuing moving of goals, adapting to a new culture, or a new CEO (the average stint they now do is reducing dramatically) is disruptive. We just get used to things and the whole cycle of change starts again.

I recently worked with a company whose new CEO wanted justification for an offsite meeting that had been happening once a quarter for the last three years and was part of the management strategy for aligning goals and motivating the management team. This team had had spectacular success with profits in double-digit growth. The head of the division, responsible for these meetings, had a strong track record for staff retention and morale while at the same time delivering a strong numbers performance. The justification the new CEO requested was so rigorous that two senior members of their team spent two days preparing the document. The new CEO had asked for justification on return on investment, yet he'd just lost two days' work from two of his top team. Goodness knows how many people they in turn had tapped to pull the information together, not to mention the loss of motivation, goodwill and energy. That sort of thing is work without meaning. It's a small, but oh so typical example that highlights the headless chicken routine as people try to get to grips with new roles and goals and are left feeling exasperated, worn out with the sure knowledge that they've just spent valuable time on something that was unnecessary, in an already too-crowded schedule.

Some years ago, I asked a client to draw a picture of his

current situation, and then one showing how he'd like his life to be. I was shocked at the results. He drew himself with a chain around his neck, being held tightly by a big hand. He had other chains chaining him to his desk, his PC and his phone. The hand represented his clients. His ideal picture was of him sitting relaxed on a sofa, in a nice environment with light bulb bubbles coming out of his head denoting creative thoughts. He had a smile on his face in the second picture, a tortured expression in the first. I could hardly believe my eyes. They say a picture paints a thousand words. Was he deadened? You betcha. Is he still with the company? No. That company lost ten years of loyal service from that employee because it would not transfer him from a client-facing deskbound position to the creative, strategic one he craved.

I ask all my clients to draw a picture to depict their position, as it helps circumvent the rationalizing, left-brain logical response that we usually trot out. I have seen some truly amazing pictures, and that's how I know that people are spinning and are deadened. It is hard to posture in a picture. The truth comes straight out.

The knowledge revolution and communication crises

It is knowledge that we need to share because that's what we now trade in. We are knowledge workers in a knowledge society where traditional factors of production and output have become secondary to knowledge. And as knowledge has become more important it has become more specialized. Everybody needs to access the knowledge of everybody else, and we know it. So what? Why does this cause a communication crisis?

Many times when I go into companies as a coach, the key issue they want to resolve is the lack of communication. I probe further. *'Tell me,'* I say, *'what is it you don't know that you want to know?'* But they don't know. They don't know what they don't know. They realize that they are scared of what they don't know. That's the trouble. When we don't know what we don't know, it gets scary because it seems so huge and so unmanageable. When I ask people to crystallize what they really need to know in order to enhance the effectiveness of their team, it suddenly comes into focus and becomes more manageable. The huge shadow of the 'don't know' becomes a clear succinct question.

There is a communication crisis in most teams and there are two central issues that are not being communicated effectively, namely *'what's my role and what's our goal?'* *'Give us some meaning,'* we cry. My role as a coach, and that of my colleagues as facilitators, is usually centred round making communication easier, helping people understand each other, encouraging them to share information. Good communication is dynamic, emotional and uniting. Bad communication is draining, hurtful and demotivating. And no communication is bad communication. The void is filled with bad and scary things, so fill the void with clear communication.

Because of the knowledge worker revolution, the need to communicate has never been so vital. But effective communication takes time and skill and, although it has become a core requirement, it is still the thing that is most overlooked when it comes to training. Few people are trained in effective time-saving communication skills. Take the example above about the new CEO wanting justification of the offsite meeting. Perhaps if he had been honest about his real concerns, or if the division head could have had a courageous conversation straight back, along the lines of *'what is this really about? What are your concerns about the offsite meeting? I don't want to wind my people up in lengthy justifications. Profits are in double-digit growth, what is it that you need to hear from me to make you comfortable that it is a good use of our time?'*, perhaps two days' work could have been saved. David Whyte, a poet and speaker who uses poetry to help people understand corporate problems, talks of having 'courageous conversations'. He makes the point that the word 'courageous' comes from the French word, *coeur*, meaning the heart. Conversations from the heart, brave ones. We need more of them.

We need to learn to talk to each other more openly, more courageously, for we are only telling half the story when we act out conversations at the tip of the iceberg. We are human, we have emotions. Why do we pretend they do not exist? When we acknowledge the whole range of our communication spectrum, we connect. And that's what makes a difference at work. We want to connect. We want to communicate with meaning and be communicated with meaningfully.

Effective communication is more vital than ever because knowledge is our core currency and we need to share it to succeed. We know this. If we take responsibility we can fight the patterns that the corporate trends are imposing on us. If communication crises, spinning and deadening are replaced with dynamic, effective communication, purposeful action and enlivening energy, then we have a better sense of choice and control at work. This is vital because the work–life balance is *more to do with how we handle work than how much of it we do*. It doesn't matter how fulfilled our life outside work is, or how few hours we work. If when we work we are spinning, deadened or poorly communicated to, we will feel out of balance.

Much talk about work–life balance points the finger of blame at the Government or the employer. Well I point my finger firmly in the direction of you. And me. It's not about them, it's about us. Once we accept the responsibility to solve this problem ourselves, from our own perspective, to look at what balance we want to achieve, only then will we have the work–life balance exactly as we want it. How is somebody else ever going to be able to solve our mystery for us satisfactorily? We have too many of the clues inside our heads, too many answers in there just waiting to be found. Taking personal responsibility for our own balance is the first step, not waiting for someone to knock on our door with it on a silver platter. *Room service, madam. Your complimentary work–life balance. And would madam like a bowl of cherries with that?* Yes, madam would. *But madam must remember to order it if she wants it.* Ask and we can receive. Don't ask . . . what are the chances?

It is all too easy for us to bemoan our situation at work and consciously or unconsciously to assume we have no choices about how we handle our days at work. My role as a coach is to remind people not to accept what they are not happy with in their work, but to do something about it. By taking the initiative, by internalizing our sense of control, we get results. In those moments of seeing progress we feel more confident about ourselves, and more convinced that our role is meaningful. I hear again and again from my clients that when work goes out of control, so does everything else. Take Duncan, a sought after TV executive, who after two health scares of blood pressure and a tumour, has decided to put work–life balance at the top of his agenda. He is not interested in downgrading his position or his hours because that isn't the answer for him. When he is on top of things at work, he leaves the office at a decent time, doesn't feel the need for a release of junk food or alcohol, so ends up eating better, going to bed earlier and then getting up earlier, ready to start the day in a positive manner. When he lets himself get out of control at work, he swings into a vicious cycle of late nights, binge eating and drinking, getting into the office late, chasing his tail all the next day, and using his frenetic work as an excuse to lead a chaotic and disorganized life. Once we identified his cycle, we were able to see where he could improve. Duncan now ensures the day works to his agenda as often as possible by arriving in his office one hour earlier and planning the day to achieve his goals. The lack of buffeting makes him feel in control and that he has choices. When he stays late, he does it through choice and it doesn't send him into the spiral of self-sabotaging behaviour. This is vital for him because work–life balance has such implications for his health.

If we want choices, freedom and a sense of control, we must take back the reins and get our lives in control. From that point, our creativity will grow, our options expand and more importantly we will find the courage to turn choices into real opportunities, not just options in the air.

SUMMARY

As the pressures of working life in the 21st century become ever more intense, huge numbers of the working population are reporting soaring levels of stress, exhaustion and frustration. The sense of feeling out of control, of staggering from one demanding situation to another, feeling crushed and unable to see the bigger picture, are all commonplace. If we want a good work–life balance, we must ensure we feel good about the work we are doing, and that we feel in control of how we handle that work. For if we can get work right, much else falls into place. We must remember that we have choices and control over how we respond to these changing times.

Trends in the workplace that are causing this imbalance can be addressed by not accepting them as a given and remembering that *the choice is ours*. We *can* develop a more conscious and controlled approach and deal more proactively with the buffeting changes in corporate life. We *can* become the buffeter.

It's a choice to spin and we must stop if it's making us sick. It's a choice to live a deadened life and we must take charge of what we need to know and seek out the answers in order to enliven ourselves. It's time to live our life purposefully, on purpose, with purpose. It's a choice to live surrounded by poor communication. Speak and listen honestly, from the heart . . . with courage. It makes us feel alive.

We *can* regain the initiative and rediscover a work–life balance that is right for us surprisingly easily. It doesn't have to be this way. Choose balance. If we want it, we can have it. Easily.

Interactive session

Dead or alive?

- Ask yourself (or get a friend or coach to ask you) what you are doing or not doing that is causing your life to be like this. Is it that you're not questioning? That you haven't told your boss what you want from your job? That you're spinning your way through every day? Are you allowing yourself to believe that this is the only way to do things?
- Make a list of the things that energize and enliven you at work, and the things that deaden you.
- Now think of how you could organize your routine to get more energizers and fewer deadeners in your day. Focus purely on the day ahead, then, when you feel ready, the week ahead, then look at the month, then the year.

Communication

- Ask your main direct reports or project leaders how they like to be communicated with. Easy and fun questions to ask are: *How can I guarantee the best from you?* and *How can I guarantee the absolute worst from you*? Both are non-threatening and will elicit a wealth of information about how to communicate effectively.

Control

- What is your external:internal locus of control ratio? What would you like it to be?
- Make a list of the situations where you feel most in control, when the locus of control is fully internalized.

- Ask yourself what it is about these situations that makes you feel like that. Is it that you have enough information, that you're feeling confident about the people involved or simply you've had enough time to think things through?
- Now think about some actions you can take to help support yourself better in situations where the locus of control becomes external. It could be ensuring time to prepare for a meeting, that you have all the necessary information, that you feel confident with a person.

Rituals

- Start each day with a ten-minute ritual on your own – it could be at a café before work, at home, on the journey to work, at your desk, in a meeting room. Ask yourself what you want to get out of the day and what do you not want from today? Get purposeful.
- Start each meeting in a similar way. What do we want from this meeting and how long is it going to last? Stay focused on the time constraint and the desired outcome. Be clear whether it's a brainstorming session, an exchange of information or a decision-making meeting.
- Regularly ask yourself or a friend or colleague: '*In what way am I choosing my current situation or state of mind?*', even when it seems incredibly unlikely that you are. For example: '*I hate this weather.*' How could you possibly be choosing the weather? Surely you

have no choice or control over it. Correct, but you do have a choice and control over how you *respond* to the weather, so the conversation might go something like this: '*In what way am I choosing this weather?*' '*Because you live here. You don't go on holiday enough and you don't dress warmly enough when it's bad, you try to be too fashion-conscious.*' You see, it's not the weather per se that you are feeling bad about, it's your inappropriate response to it. If you change your response – i.e. wear warmer clothes – you allow yourself to respond in a different way and, most importantly, prevent yourself from looking on impotently in the mistaken belief that you can do nothing about how you feel about the situation.

WHY . . .

are we out of balance?

*What's going on
in society*

?

2

The Wake-up Call

Society, I believe, is currently going through a collective mid-life crisis – or *transition*, as I prefer to call it – a time of change, development and growth. And change, as we saw in Chapter 1, is a phenomenon that knocks us out of balance as we grapple with new responses to our changing environment. The mid-life crisis is, of course, well documented as a phase in life that creeps up on individuals in the form of a sense of confusion, imbalance and disillusionment, from which is born a desire to change. Daniel Levinson, a Yale University psychologist who has conducted a study of adult life, says that as people enter their middle adulthood (usually about age 40 in males, but more linked to the family life-cycle in women), they begin to question the purpose of their existence. What have I done with my life so far? Where am I now? Of what value is my life to society, to others and especially to me? What space is there for spirituality? I believe these symptoms are very prevalent, and that they may be occurring to people outside the typical 'age' of a mid-life transition. It is more a case of experiencing the transition when you are ready. The first signs of readiness are the questioning and sense of confusion and desire for more.

My original intention here was to regale you with facts

and figures about the rise of personal development trends and spirituality to show how prevalent these trends are in society. I intended to document the growth in the number of self-development and psychology books that are published, the increasing popularity of meditation and yoga classes, and the rising interest in spirituality, as borne out by the number of books, courses and lectures on various aspects of the subject. But that all sounds rather obvious. Let's be honest, the rising numbers of people looking inwards, searching for some deeper meaning to life, be it in the form of a recognized religion, broader spirituality, meditation or alternative therapies is as clear as the nose on the end of our faces. It's there, all around us, everywhere. We are all searching for greater meaning. Instead, far more interesting is the discovery of how this phase affects the individual, and then, even more intriguing, how – and why – we are now experiencing this phase on a collective level too.

Phases of life

Some talk of life in terms of seasons, but I look at it in phases. The mid-life transition happens, in theory, around our mid-life point, though I prefer to think of it as linked to a life stage rather than age. This transition moves us into a more developmental phase of our lives. Just looking at the age aspect for a moment, the transition, for those of us who live in the west, where the average life expectancy is 75–80 years, happens at around 35–40 years of age. However, if we lived in Namibia, for example, where my husband and I took our honeymoon, we would be experiencing our mid-life transition at 21, for life expectancy in that country is only 40 years. Personally, when I consider my life against those statistics, I find it a very compelling motivator to focus on getting the second half right. It's a wake-up call that has me sitting bolt upright. The transition, however, can occur at ages outside our mid-point, often accompanying big life or world events. The importance is to notice the symptoms, and to act rather than assume you need to sit tight until you are 40 before you can move on to a more rounded phase.

This is the wake-up call

So, this is how it goes. In psychological theory, the first part of life is spent getting sorted financially, work-wise, status-wise, personality-wise and, if it's what you want, finding a partner and having a family. Then comes the mid-life, which, most psychologists agree, is a period of moving through the so-called mid-life transition and crossing the bridge into a new developmental phase characterized by a sense of fulfilment and harmony. Some psychologists refer to this fulfilled state as 'self actualization' (Maslow) or as 'individuation' (Jung). Whatever we call it, we all experience this transition differently, some of us sailing through, others battling with considerable angst. Some may experience it in their twenties, others in their sixties. But the process of questioning, of looking deep inside ourselves, is common to all, for this is a time at which we must look inside ourselves to understand who we are and how we relate to the world. In order to move forward successfully into the second part of life, we must accept ourselves in our entirety, integrating parts of our personalities – the good and the bad – that have been buried or lost or simply not allowed to develop fully. It is a time of exploration of the self and the world around us. It's essentially a spiritual process – in the broadest sense of the word – it's the search for life's meaning.

We also have to deal with a sense of loss, however, for we are unlikely to achieve this transition using the same tools that saw us through the first part of life. So it's a time of saying goodbye as well as hello. We mustn't ignore what has gone before, but we must acknowledge this as a new era, a second and different act that needs different costumes and that needs characters to grow in depth and complexity so the plot can unfurl satisfactorily.

Sadly, western societies don't have much in the way of rituals, or even education, to help people through this transition. That job has been given to psychologists and psychotherapists. Be that as it may, we should not shy away from this transition or pretend it's not there, for we can find balance by embracing it. Hear the call to start afresh, to try out new skills and behaviours and explore aspects of ourselves that we didn't really need up to now. If we don't hear the call, psychologists say, we risk being left bored, empty, inflexible and unfulfilled. Corey, another psychologist who has written about the mid-life, goes as far as saying that adults who fail to achieve productivity at this stage in life begin to experience a kind of psychological death. That sends shivers down my spine. What a thought. Corey is effectively saying that by clinging rigidly to what we have been in the first part of our life we risk having a life that is half-lived. And this is what I think our hankering for more work–life balance is all about. We want a full life. Not half a life spent nailed to the office floor.

How should we respond to the wake-up call?

Most psychologists agree that the way to a fulfilled second half, or 'afternoon of life' as Jung referred to it, is through *integrating* the neglected parts of the self and *expressing* them. So the analytical person explores creativity, the rational person explores his emotional side, and the good you, the acceptable you, has to accept that there are other bits of you that are not so acceptable too. The key is accepting these parts and not disowning them or, worse still, pretending they don't exist.

Removing our masks

This is a time for our public face, the one that we present to the world, to change into one that isn't perhaps so polished but that is more honest and more lovable for that. I think of it like the antique table in our kitchen that has a hundred scratches and marks on it, that has seen friendship and laughter, cross words, shouting and tantrums, children's painting, family meals day in, day out. It's not new, it's not polished, it's not funky, but it's loved nonetheless.

It's hard, so hard, though, to let go of our public face, our mask. We have spent years buffing and polishing it, honing and refining it, in the same way that we have spent years burying all the supposedly unacceptable bits of us. *'Please don't tell me I have to go digging them up again,'* I hear you cry. The key is to remember that these other aspects of our personality *do* exist and not to become so comfortable with our public face that we think that that is who we really are. We are never just that public face. We are always much, much more.

I recently had an invigorating and challenging session with

one of my clients. He sent me flowers the next day. He didn't say why, other than to thank me for an enjoyable session, but I knew – and he knew – the reason he'd sent them. In that session we – or rather he – had ripped away his mask. He realized that he had started to believe that this mask was his true being. *'Thank you,'* he said, *'for bringing me down a peg or two. I have been surrounding myself with cronies who tell me what I want to hear. I had lost touch with who I really am.'*

Now, my coaching style is usually one of building up rather than bringing down. But the polished persona, the mask of success of this particular client had become so shiny that he had become wedded to it, forgetting to behave with loyalty and respect and integrity to himself and others around him, forgetting who he really was. This golden boy is phenomenally successful. He is showered with material and status rewards, but things in the last month had started to go wrong for him. He'd lost his way, had started identifying too much with his public face, and failed to recognize his true self. He'd lost sight of the fact that we are multi-faceted beings, good and bad, nasty and nice, successful and hopeless. When we pretend we are just *one*, or even some, of those is when things start to go wrong. We are all. Emotions get suppressed, illnesses can start, political shenanigans get in the way of true relationships. The integrity slips and the sleepless nights creep in. The surefooted path becomes a wobbling lurch of mistaken judgement calls and faltering relationships. *'Get back on track,'* I said to my client. *'Remember your integrity, play with a straight bat, and don't fall too deeply in love with your public persona, because it's only part of your story. You are more than that. Embrace the whole.'*

Even as we are busy polishing our masks, we still long for a real connection with people and, when it happens, it feels fantastic. The puffery and the empty words are replaced by meaningful looks and a sense of understanding. I recently conducted a workshop for two teams in the same company who were heavily in conflict and, despite instructions from the CEO for them to behave collaboratively, were determined to compete against each other in the race of 'thunderstealing', as I call it. *'Masks off,'* I said, *'let's have real people in the room, warts and all. We all have unpleasant characteristics, let's just face up to them. Why is it so important to win?'*

And we started to question. Why is stealing that thunder so very important? What will we do with it when we get it home? Thunder in the bedroom makes for a sleepless night. Within an hour of facilitated talk the masks were off, the tension had dissipated, the smiles had become genuine, the bodies relaxed. Closed gestures were replaced with expansive body language; the eye contact was inclusive. We're in this together, it said, we want the same things, harmony, connection, communication. Let's make it happen. Let's turn our inward eyes outward and compete together against the world out there. That's the race to win.

So why do we find it so hard to talk like that? Because we are all wearing our masks. Take them off every now and again – or at least remember they are there – and see what happens.

What's under the mask?

Remove the mask and we uncover the side of ourselves that contains those nasty bits, the bits we'd rather not show the world, or that we have learned to keep hidden away. The volatility of a child's emotions gives a clue as to what we might look like with our masks off. Their existence is one of mood swings, tantrums and furies followed by dancing delights, brutal honesty and hurtful truths, of jumping and leaping, and energy fizzing over. As adults we are influenced by the culture in which we live, by our parents and wider families, our friends, schools and work. We wise up pretty quickly as to what we feel should be hidden and what should be on show.

But the key to healthy personal development, and an easy ride through the transition phase, many psychologists claim, is to accept and integrate the parts of our personalities that, on the face of it, are less acceptable to society. These parts may not be all bad or difficult, however. Some are pure treasure. Indeed, it is generally accepted that for some people it is actually harder to acknowledge and integrate the positive personality traits than it is the negative ones, because what really scares us is often not how awful we can be, but how amazing we can be. Our power and potential scare us. In my experience, this is often the hardest part of the mid-life transition: the acceptance of our potential greatness and the move from the comfort zone of known and familiar behaviours toward something new and potentially discomforting.

The comfort zone

The place where I talk with my clients is an intimate one. It allows them to be more themselves; it enables me to see the treasure in them, the potential and the astounding talents. When I mirror these qualities back to my clients or encourage them not to keep such a tight rein on them, I see and hear fear. Often, the world they are in is too comfortable, too nice. Their colleagues are too much fun, the pay is too high, it's too dangerous to risk the security of it all just because a little malaise, disillusionment or under-performance has crept in.

They rationalize loud and clear, terrifying themselves with their use of powerful images so that the comfort zone with its inherent images of safety nets and blankets, is discussed in the same breath as being in the line of fire, of raising heads above parapets, of jumping off cliffs and rocking boats. *'Go on,'* I laugh, *'try terrifying yourself even more.'* Who in their right mind would leave warmth and safety to be shot at, or jump from a great height or fall out of a boat? And so the status quo wins the day.

Or rather, living the half-life wins the day. The true fire in the belly is quelled, the sparkle in the eyes, the animated gestures are dampened in a sunken physiology as my clients insist they can't or won't leave their blankets and the warmth, because they fear they may die. Believe me, we won't die if we do embrace this change – but that psychological death that Corey wrote about may creep up on us if we don't.

Change does not necessarily mean we have to leave the company, drop out, or even downshift. It's more a case of exploring and trying out new things, testing out other aspects of our behaviour, integrating some of the lost treasure into our lives, or some of the darker bits. These are the things that make us whole. Leaving them untouched or unexplored sends us winging back into the half-life territory. Exploring them is a natural and normal part of human development.

Let's take our dreams off the back burner. Put them to the front. Give them a stir, heat them up, see how much tastier they can be. *'How?'* my clients ask. Well, here's a way that requires just simple tasks each day that in a relatively short time will enable you to wake up and find yourself well on your journey towards a fulfilled life.

1) Break down dreams or explorations into mini-steps

A dream is made of many facets. The clearer you can imagine each facet, the greater the chance of it becoming an actuality. Thought creates reality. The first step is to write down every aspect of the dream. I like to draw a circle and inside randomly write everything about the dream that I can think of. Here's an example:

Dream: Running A School

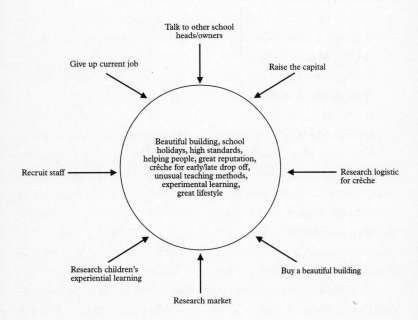

Then, on the outside of the circle, draw arrows to actions that would make particular facets of the dream happen. For example, research children's experiential learning, buy a beautiful building, raise the capital, give up current job, research market, talk to other school heads/owners, recruit staff, research logistics for crèche, and so on. Then group these into no more than six macro themes, i.e. 1) researching market, 2) financing the project, 3) getting prerequisite training and credentials, 4) leaving current job, 5) legal aspects of childcare/crèche, 6) property. Once you have your macro themes, list, under each one, three easy steps you could take that would move you nearer to that goal. DO NOT TRY AND SOLVE THE WHOLE THING IN ONE STEP – it is too daunting!

So, taking the example of researching market, three easy steps could be:

a) Make a list of all the schools I admire.
b) List what it is I admire about them.
c) Get the phone numbers, addresses or Web addresses of all these schools.

These are do-able. Probably, even, thoroughly enjoyable!

The aim is to have three steps for each macro theme, making 18 easy actions in total. These steps, as suggested above, could be as simple as a phone call, a chat with a friend, drawing up a list, searching the Web or cutting out an article. Remember, NO ACTION IS TOO SMALL! Do one small action like that – and it must be an *action* – each day for 18 days. That's it.

Then, after 18 days, take a look. It is staggering how effortlessly the back of that journey towards our dreams has been broken. Once you've done those 18 days your journey will gain its own momentum.

When we stand at the top of our imagined cliff and think of the enormous, terrifying leap we need to make to reach our dream, we become paralysed. I work constantly with clients breaking down their cliffs into mini-steps down the equivalent of a sturdy and safe rope ladder. One small step at a time. Consistently, clients claim that this is the single most helpful technique in moving them forward to achieving their dreams. After years of paralysis, those small steps are tiny but hugely significant triumphs.

2) Change language

Our language is the coding of our thought. If we change our language, our thoughts will change with it. Paint a picture internally that creates a pleasant image for both the comfort zone we are in and the other end of the spectrum, so that we are not creating a terrifying polarity through language. That way we are offering ourselves real choice. So, for example, if the status quo is a comfort zone where living is easy, we should make the alternative image of following our dreams something like being a role model for our children, or the opening of a flower, a bursting of creativity. Intention and focus, that's all it needs. We don't even have to be brave, just committed. Commitment to the two strategies outlined above proves our desire to enter the transitionary phase willingly. We're on the road towards fulfilment and away from psychological death.

Role models

We can support our decision by focusing on some role models. Picking some that have made a success (in the way we perceive success) while following their dreams, hobbies or interests. We can all find such role models, people who are following their interests within large companies (hubs, project groups, roving briefs, project management, joint ventures and entrepreneurial divisions) and of course outside mainstream companies in the world of business start-ups. The role models are there if we open our eyes to them.

I was coaching a senior executive who wanted a different, broader, group role in her company, a role that currently didn't exist. She kept telling me how there was no precedent for anything like it. Nobody changed roles, nobody moved departments or divisions, and nobody ever had roles created for them. Apparently. As I knew the company very well I was able to challenge her view and give her four or five examples immediately of people who had done exactly that. We agreed a plan where she would start to look for more examples and go and discuss with these other people how they had gone about changing their role. If you open your eyes and let the right role models in it is possible to prove your dream can work rather than focusing on how it has never been done before. If we don't open our eyes, our dreams will be rejected and we will find ourselves firmly back in our restrictive box.

Another of my clients, a very successful career woman who was the main breadwinner in her family, wanted to leave mainstream industry and follow some of her interests. *'But,'* she said, *'nobody that I know who has started a business doing something creative or what they believe in, has ever made any money.'* I was flabbergasted. I live in that world, I am one of those people. I encouraged her to shift her filtering mechanisms, to start creating a mental file called *entrepreneurs, people who love what they do and make money*. She slowly started to add some names to that file. In doing so she reduced in visual size and importance the amorphous mental folder that said *entrepreneurs, people who love what they do and are poor as church mice*, which previously had dominated her mental screen. This had continually proved to her that her dreams were unobtainable. This client is still in mainstream industry, but now has an 'exit strategy' for three years time. This keeps her motivated. She keeps her focus on what's possible, not what's impossible.

If we shift our focus on to role models that prove our dream is possible, we are paving the way for success rather than failure. Importantly, we are paving the way for change.

Waking up to change

Is it so bad, though, to stay in the comfort zone? No, of course not, as long as it's a conscious choice and you are happy there. May you stay comfy for ever more. I know somebody like this who has been in the same job in the same company for 20 years. That's quite a rarity in itself these days, but perhaps even more rare is that he is genuinely delighted to go to work each day, he loves what he does. And everyone around him can see it. He is at peace with himself. All is well. He has done his explorations within his role, he is more sociable, he has conquered much of his shyness, he attends more corporate events and talks to people he doesn't know. All those are new behaviours for him.

Studies have shown that five per cent of the population only seek major change in their work life every 15 years or so. Most of us are on a five- to seven-year cycle before the change bell starts ringing. For a fifth of us, the bell rings every one or two years (this is borne out from the work by Rodger Bailey in the USA that looked at our filters for wanting sameness and difference in our work). Wake-up calls and ringing bells are there to help us achieve our full potential, to develop fully and, personally, I think it's great that we are feeling so unsettled by it, that we do feel out of balance, because this is the chance for a life of balance to be fully lived. The changes are a call to action. They tell us it's time to counterbalance the feeling of imbalance felt in the early stages of this transitional phase.

But why are we feeling this call so strongly right now? I believe four external factors are acting as the strongest catalysts:

- the changing role of work
- the religious void in our lives
- the ageing population
- earlier acquisition of material wealth.

The changing role of work

In the previous chapter we talked about some of the trends causing the imbalance. The workplace has become the place where people are asked to do more and more without really understanding why. If we are senior enough to understand why, it can become meaningless in any case as we search for more personal meaning to our lives. We search and we will find. It is the human purpose, the human way. We are not made to come and work with no purpose. The role of work has been widely documented in psychological and sociological studies as so much more than somewhere just to earn a wage. So much is tied up in it, our role, our status, our self-esteem, the laughs, the play and the creativity. So what happens when it goes a bit awry, when the sparkle goes?

We need to remind ourselves why we are here. We are here as humans with a heart, and a soul, a spirit. We must find a way to connect back with our purpose, to do things that deeply move us or others – and, all being well, both. The money contract is now supplemented with an emotional contract but if our employer does not honour that emotional contract, disillusionment grows. The contract is: *Keep me interested, keep me developing, tell me I make a difference, let me really see and feel and hear my contribution, let me feel that what I'm doing is important and worthwhile. Oh, and reward me fairly for what I do.* Break the contract, break the trust and watch disillusionment take a seat at the board-room table.

There is disillusionment in the ranks of the 'have it all but have nothing' brigade. The disillusioned employee sighs: '*I have everything, yet nothing to impart. I am too tired, I am too lost in it. I have stifled my creativity, filed away my dreams in the too-difficult basket.*' Just as a restaurant nowadays cannot be just a place to eat but must also offer an experience, a buzz, make a statement, so our careers must do more than pay us a monthly wage to cover our bills. It is not enough to be fed and watered. We want, need and expect more. What was once perceived as the norm is no longer enough and as disillusionment sets in sooner, the once-thrilling career leaves employees either lazy and frustrated, or so stressed by the pressures that they are too crazed to stop and think. They flop in the evenings and then stay awake half the night not allowing the restorative patterns of sleep and dreams to do their work.

The good news is that disillusionment and a sense of confusion or loss are often the first indication that the transitionary period is upon us. Why is that good news? Because out of confusion comes clarity, out of disillusionment comes action and out of loss comes some new beginnings and a sense of positive nostalgia for all that has gone before.

The trends in the workplace are causing us to look at new ways of working. Because of the rise of the small business culture and the myriad ways we can now work within a company, the opportunity to explore and be more open about our developmental needs has resulted in more exposure to and awareness of what's going on in people's heads. *'I want to work in a different way'* is becoming an acceptable thing to say to our bosses. The entrepreneurial culture, so elegantly captured in Charles Handy's book *The Elephant and the Flea*, suggests that this pattern is here to stay. The dotcom culture, the start-up, the symbiotic relationship of the elephants (big companies) and the fleas (the small businesses and one-man bands), are making it OK to explore, take risks, try out new ways of working. Because, remember, our work is not just about how much we are paid, it's linked into our self-esteem and our happiness. Work is an outlet for us to explore our personalities, relationships, creativity and our contribution to the world. Work is a rich part of life, and an integral part of a successful work–life balance.

The religious void

By turning away from conventional religion, as we have done as a society over recent years, we have been left with a gaping hole in our lives; we have no sense of higher purpose or trust in higher powers. The result? We are now looking for something to fill the void – for it needs to be filled in order to make us whole – and are finding ourselves looking inwards, searching for more spirituality in our lives.

Studies have shown that people with a faith in something bigger than them, be it God or some other form of spirituality, can cope with grief, illness and, indeed, with life better than those who don't. Study after study has shown that the presence of a chaplain can decrease hospitalization time by 20 per cent or more. Recovery rates are more rapid when religious or spiritual beliefs play a part. In a study reported in the *American Journal of Psychiatry*, H.G. Koenig (et al) found that depressed patients who had a strong religious faith recovered over 70 per cent faster from depression than those with less strong faith. The same researcher also published an article in the *International Journal of Psychiatry in Medicine* in the late 1990s, which showed that frequent churchgoers had stronger immune systems than less frequent ones. He followed a sample of almost 2,000 older adults over six years and found that the frequent churchgoers had lower plasma interlukin levels than their less religious counterparts, indicating a healthier and stronger immune system. Other studies connect spirituality and religion to longer life expectancy and better wellbeing.

We like to believe in something. It's the way we are meant to be. Even the earliest works of literature, from every part of the world, refer to the worshipping of gods, goddesses or spirits. It's just something we do. Or should do. Take it away and we are left with a strange sense of a rudderless ship, a company with no leader. It's as if the Chief Executive (CEO) has gone and the financial director has been put in as acting CEO and we're following him because we like to have a sense of where to go. But our commitment remains tempered as we wait for a new CEO to be appointed. When he comes, we kid ourselves, we'll know where we're going. Then, tired of waiting, we eventually look elsewhere for direction. Whether people choose a community-based spiritual commitment, or they follow a personal journey alone, it is essentially the same yearning for greater meaning. Traditional churchgoing is declining steeply in the UK but if you look to the USA where there is high energy and a sense of vitality in the church, that statistic is reversed and churchgoers are increasing in number. In fact, almost half of Americans and a quarter of Australians go to church, whereas less than a tenth of the population of Britain attends.

It's normal, it's natural, and there is excitement around spirituality and the new church and interfaith ministries across the western world. We are finding our way back to a connection, because we need to, because we're human and humans need 'god' figures or a sense of something bigger than us to fill the void and make us whole. Whether this takes the form of revisiting ancient religions and cultures or exploring newer forms of spirituality, it's all part of the human psyche that needs and wants to have someone or something to look up to, to follow, to adore, to respect, to trust and to ask for help.

Earlier material wealth

In the west, we now acquire material wealth much earlier in our lives than people did a generation back. Technological advances have given us labour-saving devices galore and we are able to buy into them far sooner than our parents could. Central heating, washing machines, dishwashers, microwaves, TVs, radios and telephones have a staggeringly high penetration in western households, connecting us, saving us time and speeding up our lives.

So what? When Maslow first published his now-famous hierarchy of needs in the 1950s, it was on the assumption that it would take a significant proportion of our life before we'd even start worrying about the top of the pyramid. *We won't start worrying about self-actualization if we're still concerned about where our next meal is coming from,* was the premise. Now, however, we meet our basic needs far earlier in our lives, leaving the way open to deal with self-actualization in our thirties or, for some of us, even our twenties.

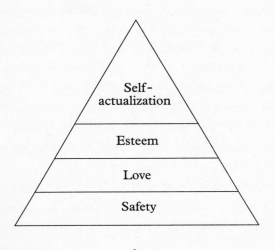

In fact with growing documentation of a so-called quarter-life crisis, which happens to people in their twenties, we are witnessing the younger generation's fascination with self-actualization at earlier and earlier stages. They have witnessed some of the extremities in working patterns and seen the mistakes of older generations and are determined to have a rounder, fuller life, earlier. The relevance of this social trend to our awareness of the mid-life transition becomes evident in the light of the fourth catalyst, the fact that the changing demographics mean there are more older people than ever before. As a result, more people are dealing with these issues than ever before.

Ageing population

More than a third of the population is between 30 and 50 years old, and the population is ageing. The increasing size of this group means there's now a mass interest in the issues that the mid-life transition throws up, such as personal development and a search for greater, deeper meaning in life. It's contagious because there are more people thinking about it and talking about it than ever before. This catalyst is key to the reason why this mid-life transition, as I mentioned at the beginning of the chapter, is being felt on a *collective* level in western society as well as on an *individual* level. The convergence of such powerful social and demographic trends as the ones outlined above has turned what used to be an individual transition, a personal experience, into one that has become more public and more widely documented.

This wake-up call to cross the bridge into the next part of our lives, to make the next step in our journey towards full and healthy development as human beings, is being heard by more people at the same time than ever before. We do not have to live out the entire first half of our life out of balance before we can do something about it. The transition comes when we are ready. And the first signs of readiness are the stress, confusion and dissatisfaction that come from falling out of balance. So if we feel those things, we can act now. Disequilibrium is the first glorious sign that we are, potentially, on the road to a fuller, healthier, more rounded life. If we choose to see it that way.

But why should it matter what the person next door to us, or in the same office is experiencing? Why are we finding ourselves so affected by the experiences of others? Because we're all linked.

Systemic thinking

Systemic thinking is a psychological term used to describe ways of looking at a situation in its entirety, viewing it as part of a bigger *system* rather than in isolation: we can't look at one family member's behaviour, for example, without taking into account the system (the family) they come from and operate in. This theory is used extensively in companies, working from the premise that all parts of an organization are related so that behaviour patterns in one part impact on the entire organization. It means that if some key members start behaving in certain ways, *it affects us all*. In our system that is society, we will feel the reverberations if powerful members of the system, such as the media, government, royalty or celebrities start to speak or behave in certain ways. It triggers a response in us. We do not and cannot operate in isolation. Let me give you two very simple examples that relate to my own experience:

- When I decided to leave the company I'd worked for for many years, I became drawn to other people that worked in a non-traditional way. Now I, in turn, attract people who are interested in working in a non-traditional way. They have open and honest conversations with me. They talk to me because they trust me, telling me things they may not tell anyone else. They can see I've made the move, so I am unlikely to pour scorn on their own ideas and dreams. *The way I behave affects how other people interact with me.*

- After setting up my own company I became very outspoken with clients on the importance of a balanced life. With my own life clearly more in balance, my attitude and talk changed and I now attract a similar attitude, with the result that clients no longer tell me how frantically busy they are, but delight in reporting how they leave work on time, spend mornings writing a document in a park, or take time to have a massage in the middle of the day. *Again, my behaviour affects how people interact with me. I do not operate in isolation.*

This is also known as the *observer effect.* When an observer – me in the case of my coaching sessions, or, on a wider scale, a key figure in society – is present he and his views and behaviours are variables that must be taken into account because there is no such thing as objective reality. We create our own reality based on what we are looking for. It depends on what we filter in and out and that in turn is based on what we *want* to hear or notice. So, when key figures in our social system, i.e. those with the loudest voices – celebrities, presidents, royalty or the media – speak out on such subjects as spirituality, meditation, complementary medicine, alternative therapies, yoga or religion, we start to believe. It is our interaction and engagement with the observer's views that creates our reality.

Margaret Wheatley in her breakthrough book, *Leadership and the new sciences*, argues that organizations are living, breathing, self-renewing systems. At one point in the book she asks: '*Which is the more important influence, the individual or the system?*' Her answer is: '*It depends*', because it is the *relationship* between these two that is critical and, as she goes on to say, that relationship is always different depending on the players and the moment. One shift and we all start shifting. We don't all have to agree, we don't all have to adopt the same view, but we all feel the reverberations. It is no wonder we feel out of balance. The wake-up call is being experienced personally and in society. It's time for change, time to experiment and time to grow. Let us not shy away. Let us embrace it for genuine work–life balance will come from a life fully lived in which the second part balances the first.

Linked as we are, we are *all* feeling the onslaught of the external factors that are propelling us towards our mid-life transition. Many of the louder voices in our system are showing an increased interest in personal development and spirituality and such is their influence that awareness of this transitional phase is exploding into our collective consciousness with the determination of a wake-up alarm call. We mustn't press the snooze button. We may fall back to sleep, and wake up feeling it's too late in the day to get going. But don't forget, we risk dying Corey's psychological death if we do that. Let the sunlight stream in and let the new day begin because a life that embraces this natural transition, enabling dreams to be pursued and a more meaningful life to be achieved, offers some real benefits, not least of which are better energy and a greater sense of personal and professional fulfilment.

As this new stage in our lives dawns, if we face it confidently we will start to see more clearly what it promises. Our bleary eyes will focus and our staggering gait will be steadied by a sense of purpose. For true balance to occur, I believe we must cleanse last night away and respond with open arms to this wake-up call. It's time to try something new. It's time to change. It's time to rebalance.

SUMMARY

The journey towards work–life balance requires us to go through a transition phase, a transition which carries all the symptoms of the well-documented 'mid-life crisis', but which can occur at any time. We must be prepared to lift ourselves out of our comfort-zone, to accept change, and embrace aspects of ourselves that have hitherto been ignored or not fully developed. We must acknowledge our ambitions and desires, and strive to achieve them, for a balanced life is one that is fulfilled on every level.

We're not alone in embarking on this journey. Changing demographics mean that more people than ever before are reaching the stage in life at which such questioning typically starts. Society as a whole is going through the same process. We must take advantage of the momentum that that creates to make our individual journey to balance a smooth and ultimately successful one.

Interactive session

Life targets

- What has the first part of your life achieved, what do you still want to achieve?
- What do you want to achieve in the remainder of your life?
- What rebalancing needs to happen for you to live your life *fully*?
- What images/metaphors/analogies do you use to describe your life now and the life you want to lead?

Self-image

- What are the parts of you that you are hiding, which need 'honouring', both the good and the bad?
- What does your current 'mask' say about you?
- What does your mask NOT say about you?

Rituals

Dreams

- Break down your dreams into the six macro themes as outlined in the chapter, with three mini-steps for each, creating 18 mini-steps that are EASILY actionable. Do one action a day for 18 days towards your dream.
- Create a powerful compelling language about your dream. Do not scare yourself with negative images. Then talk or think about your dream with positive images and language each day.
- Focus on positive role models who are living proof that your dream is possible.

Stretch

- Practise exploring your talents, stretch yourself by doing something you wouldn't do naturally . . . regularly.

WHY . . .
are we out of balance?

What's going on
with our changing
gender roles

3

Rebalancing Energies

Do you remember at school learning the word 'homeostasis'? It is a biological term that refers to the way in which every organic system – i.e. anything with life – keeps itself in balance despite changes in its environment: how a tree develops buds, leaves and then loses its leaves; how a bear hibernates through cold weather; how a horse develops a thick coat in winter. In fact it can be observed at all levels of existence. Our whole world is one big homeostatic, self-regulating system. We self-regulate on a personal level in the same way, and we are a self-regulating race. When things get too far out of balance we compensate by going the other way – think of the baby booms and increase in male births in the wake of wars.

In the previous chapter we looked at the need to self-regulate through our lives by balancing our first half of life with our second. My belief, as I outlined previously, is that as the world's population grows older and the number of people experiencing life transition increases (almost half the workforce will be over 45 in the next ten years), world consciousness is shifting its focus on to more spiritual and cultural matters. Not because the over 45s are the only people driving this, but because so many of us are thinking it. Its contagious. In fact, in many ways the younger generation are the drivers, as they are proactively seeking a form of spirituality that works for them, that can help them create a deeper meaning in their lives. Healthy transition involves rebalancing and compensating and I believe this is what we are doing on a collective level. We are rebalancing a society that has become too 'masculine' – the term here refers to masculine *energy* – and we are now looking to rebalance by increasing the *feminine* energy within our society.

That each of us has masculine and feminine energy within us is a point long accepted by psychologists and religious thinkers. *Masculine* energy manifests itself in power, action, competitiveness, rational thinking, protection and doing, and is epitomized by the metaphor of the warrior. *Feminine* energy is represented by receptivity, intuition, nurturing, passivity, relationship-building, connections and being, and is epitomized by the metaphor of the goddess.

Masculine	Feminine
power	receptivity
action	relationship building
aggression	nurturing
competitiveness	collaborative
rational	intuitive
protection	responsive
doing	being
THE WARRIOR	THE GODDESS

A man has both masculine and feminine energy, just as a woman has both masculine and feminine energy. For most people, the cultural norm influences how much of that energy is displayed, especially in the workplace. Workplaces often have a very distinctive masculine or feminine culture where appropriate behaviours that match the culture are rewarded.

Our society and culture has developed rewarding the masculine energy. The emphasis has been on productivity, materialism, territorial aggression, and scientific and rational explanations of the world. There have obviously been extraordinary strides in human development during the masculine-dominated centuries, but, like anything done to excess, the masculine energy needs to be balanced. Masculine energy without its counterbalancing feminine force creates a world that is too busy, too aggressive and too strong, that lacks the softer, more receptive, collaborative feminine force.

Dr Fritjof Capra, author of *The Turning Point*, which has been hailed as one of the most important books of the decade on this subject, argues that the masculine/patriarchal system has led to '*a profound cultural imbalance which lies at the very root of our current crisis, an imbalance in our thoughts and feelings, our values and attitudes, and our social and political structures*'. He sees the rise of yin (feminine) energy, as he refers to it, as a self-regulatory mechanism to rebalance us.

In every man and every woman there is the yin and yang, the animus and the anima, the masculine and the feminine. Females can enjoy this feminization of society, and perhaps lose some of the masculine traits they felt they needed previously to propel them forward in the workplace. They can, if it feels right, let up being the warrior and remember to be the goddess every now and again. For men, experiencing and allowing their feminine energies to come to the fore allows them to enjoy the personality traits that better suit today's world – more listening, more collaboration, more relationship-building. These are traits that are going to make everyone a winner. Remember – the rise of the feminine spirit is about enhancing both femininity *and* masculinity, because it's about rebalancing.

The rise of feminine energy

Now, however, the *feminine archetype* – by which I mean *all things feminine* rather than the female per se – is in the ascendance. The dictionary definition of an archetype is a 'prototype', meaning an original, or model upon which things are based and when I use the term I refer to our deep understanding of what the feminine model represents, what she looks and feels like, how she behaves and what her role is. In a sense, it refers to the stereotype that pervades our consciousness.

I believe feminine energy is increasing in order to enhance our development as a race. It is increasing in both men and women and these qualities are becoming sought-after and valued in a way not previously witnessed. Up until now many businesswomen have been just as guilty of subverting their feminine side as men, but now western society is starting to play by more feminine rules, not necessarily because women are becoming more powerful, but because the feminine *archetype* is becoming more powerful and is seeping into all aspects of our lives.

Companies that specialize in looking at cultural trends call this the 'feminization' of society. My research took me to an international company that specializes in 'semiotics', the science of understanding images and symbols. The company analyses what we are receiving as input through all our senses, what we see, hear, taste, feel on a day to day basis, and then how we make sense of all this input. For when we take in information, we need to categorize it to make sense of it. We do this through language, which in turn creates our thought, for we think in the language we've learnt and this language is by definition imbued with our cultural norms. When we see images that are square, strong, mono-coloured, angular, boxed in or straight, we will interpret these images as 'masculine'; when we see images that are organic, free flowing, colourful, curvy, smaller, we will tend to attribute feminine status to these images.

This company, Semiotic Solutions, has been claiming 'feminization' as a major paradigm shift for many years. They believe it to have been in ascendancy since the 1960s, and furthermore believe it shows no sign of waning. Monty Alexander, a semiotician who travels the world predicting and evidencing these paradigm shifts, cites examples of the feminine principle being in ascendancy in China and Japan as well as North America and Europe. Alexander also highlights the difference between cultural perception and reality, meaning that whilst we may be aware of the rise of the feminine energy, either consciously or unconsciously, it may not yet be in line with reality. For example, because it takes a generation for a paradigm shift to happen, women continue to be paid less than men, and still have unequal status in the boardroom. What I am referring to here is the *perception* of changing trends in our culture. For Alexander, such trends are the little waves that echo what he calls the 'big wave that is the cultural shift of masculinization to feminization'.

These 'little waves' are already reflected in design trends.

Alexander enjoys the case of the overnight success of the i-Mac computer in a market that was dominated by design that was boxy, grey and square (masculine). i-Mac turned this market on its head by using curvy, colourful (feminine) design. He also cites the trend in car design towards smaller, curvier shapes; and the changing trends in typography used in editorial, advertisements and brands to show irregular margins, flowing writing or free-flowing layouts. These are all typically feminine traits and subliminally tell us this energy is on the increase.

In our homes and on our streets we witness daily (albeit subliminally) the increase in feminine energy in design. All these changes are cues that are feeding into our collective understanding and growing appreciation of a more feminine energy in our culture. The same can be seen in business. Collaboration, partnerships and alliances abound in business. *Empowering* as opposed to *dominating* is considered a desirable leadership style; just *being* is becoming as fashionable as *doing*; *listening* has become a new business tool; and *win-win* is heralded as the ultimate way to negotiate or resolve conflicts. All of these attitudes are 'feminine' traits, either because of basic biological differences between the sexes or because of social conditioning.

Gender differences

Competitiveness

Psychological experiments have looked at the differences in competitiveness between men and women and have found when looking at biological responses (heart rate and blood pressure) that men showed higher blood pressure when they lost than when they won, while women showed the oppo-site. Does this mean that men, with their innate sense of competitiveness, feel they are losing out with the rise of the feminine archetype? After all, some may reason, if feminine *power* is rising, *women per se* might be perceived as 'winning', and if someone is winning, then someone must, by defini-tion, be losing.

It isn't, of course, like that at all. Nobody is losing with the rise in feminine energy. On the contrary, it creates an opportunity for all to win, grow and develop, for women to reconcile themselves with their feminine values and not subvert them, and for men to flex and develop new skills. There need be no losers here. Everyone can benefit from the rise of the feminine archetype. The only loss that will occur is if we don't do something to claim a better quality of life. Many of us are desperately looking for more balance in our lives, wanting things to calm down, to soften. Caring for our families, children, parents, friends, is becoming more important than the money we hardly have time to spend. Relationship-building, long the currency primarily of females, is becoming the currency of everyone.

Virtually every month there are headlines in the business sections of newspapers about high-profile senior executives, both male and female, who have decided to give up highly paid positions to spend more time with their family or to pursue a passion or hobby. 'Life is too short,' they explain. Life is only too short if we stagnate in our development within it. If we have met our needs of biological and social security in the first part of our lives it is only natural to move on to the next developmental stage, the stage that is more spiritual, more caring. Call it individuation, call it self-actualization, call it maturing – whatever we call it, it is a natural requirement for healthy and happy human development. With material success arriving so much earlier, coupled with the ageing population, we are experiencing this stage as a race with more mass and momentum than ever before. Meeting our needs for more nurturing, for more meaningful relationships, for more spiritual meaning, for more 'feminine' values, is natural. Our lives become plenty long enough then, because we are doing what we are meant to be doing. Everybody wins.

Many psychological and gender experiments have demonstrated differences between men and women. The wars rage about whether the differences are of biological or social making and, as with many of these either/or arguments, it's a bit of both. By outlining here some of the gender differences, I hope to highlight how the skills that are becoming more valued are ones that are typically associated with females, regardless of whether your belief is that they are of biological or social making.

Differences in the brain – multi-tasking

Women's brains tend to have a larger corpus callosum than men. This is the piece of the brain that straddles the two hemispheres, connecting the two sides. Logical, analytical, rational, linear thinking is associated with the left hemisphere, and creative, intuitive, non-linear with the right. Women's brains have been shown in 'brain imaging' experiments to access more of both sides when listening, whereas men mostly access their left side. The larger corpus callosum and the swift accessing of both sides of the brain is usually used to explain the proven ability of women to concentrate on multiple tasks more successfully than many men. A television programme popularized this concept when it asked men to multi-task in a given time-scale – to iron a shirt, cook the dinner and put on some washing. The men struggled while the women found it a breeze.

This ability makes some women feel they are not using their full potential if they are only doing one thing at a time. On a grander level, this is being borne out by the female race at large where, not content with one role – that of home-maker – the innate urge to fulfil potential has moved women into acquiring the skills of their male counterparts. Does this mean women suddenly lose their homemaking skills and urges? No, they decide to add it on to the list of can-dos, want-to-dos, must-dos and should-dos. In their capacity to multi-task they often over-extend themselves – and this can often result in imbalance.

Differences in the brain – moral dilemmas
Carol Gilligan, a Harvard psychologist, used the pioneering studies of Lawrence Kohlberg (another Harvard psychologist) to show the differences between men and women in moral reasoning. While Kohlberg had focused on male responses, Gilligan explored how both sexes responded to the following situation:

A man has a wife who is dying but can only be saved by an expensive drug invented by a local druggist. The man cannot afford the drug or get credit to purchase it. Do you think the man should steal the drug to save his dying wife?

Gilligan found that males would tend to decide quickly that the man should *steal the drug*, reasoning that life has a higher value than property. In contrast, females were more likely to be worried about the impact of that action on the people involved: what would happen if the man were caught, how would that then affect his wife? They were more likely to suggest the pharmacists *donate the drugs*, or the man *borrows money*.

The female emphasis is on solutions that are beneficial to everyone. And, rather than being seen as weak or avoiding the issue, approaches which focus on a win-win solution are now considered successful strategies in negotiation and conflict-resolution in the business world.

Differences in the brain – emotional intelligence

'Emotional intelligence' (the credible proof of a different type of intelligence coined in the mid-90s by author Daniel Goleman) has entered the business lexicon as an admired way of behaving at work. There is an increasing acceptance in the workplace of the importance of improving human relations, expressing emotions, listening and empathizing. Social skills have never been higher on the agenda, and they are qualities historically associated with females. Goleman proved that the higher the emotional intelligence (EQ), the more effective the leader. The good news about emotional intelligence is that it can be learned and that it seems gradually to improve and increase with age. Goleman claims there is no gender difference overall because women are better at social skills and empathy, whereas men are better at self-confidence and resilience under stress and these four qualities are the core competencies of emotional intelligence.

Other studies have found similar gender differences. The 'father' of sociobiology, Edward O. Wilson of Harvard University, found that females tend to rate more highly than males in empathy, verbal skills, social skills and security-seeking, while men rate more highly in independence, dominance, spatial and mathematical skills, rank-related aggression. Another study by psychologist D. Kimura showed that women were better than men in human relations, in recognizing emotional overtones in others, and in language and emotional expressiveness.

As we move into a period where feminine traits are more respected, and where 'right-brain' thinking is more acceptable, and indeed in many cases becoming more appreciated, you could argue that the female brain with its biological differences in certain areas is able to respond more easily to the new criteria that constitute business success. This in part explains why the rise of the feminine archetype, although a rebalancing process, is actually knocking us out of balance. We are experiencing shifts in the balance of power and shifts in roles and those shifts can feel uncomfortable.

The rise of the feminine spirit – where are we now?

When we focus on the subject, it is impossible to doubt that the feminine spirit is on the rise as there are obvious signs for all to see. Girls have been doing better at school for many years; the number of women entering university has steadily risen, and there are now more women leaving with a degree than men; more women are in full-time employment; there are more women board-members than ever before; and more successful women are seeing their femininity as an asset, not a drawback. Young women see equal status as the norm, even if this is not yet borne out in the reality of corporate life.

So have we now reached the point at which the rise of feminine power has rebalanced our society? As yet, no. We are still in the process of rebalancing, of making the mental and physical adjustments required to regain balance. Monty Alexander, the semiotician who predicts and analyses such trends, claims the breakthrough has already happened, but that the rise will continue steadily. It is my belief that the rise of this energy is part of a self-regulating mechanism that is naturally found in all living organisms, and it is creating balance in our organizations and in our world. We need the change for the sake of healthy growth and development as a balanced culture. The changes are natural and are not a threat to either gender. Furthermore, I believe that the process is a cyclical one because we will self-regulate again if we go too far towards feminine energy, though I believe we have a very long way to go before the scales tip back the other way. So now we are at the stage where it feels confusing and some-what difficult. Good news, as this is when we can start to rebalance ourselves.

The ripple effect

Imagine a still pond, into which is thrown a tiny stone. The ripples that emanate have increasingly large circles, wholly disproportionate to the size of the stone. The rise of the femi-nine spirit is like those ripples. The first ripple is the impact felt on a personal level by men and women. The growing prominence of women in the workplace necessitates dealing with issues of guilt and balancing work and home life in a way never before experienced. As men and women grapple with their changing roles we see the ripple effect move into society as a whole.

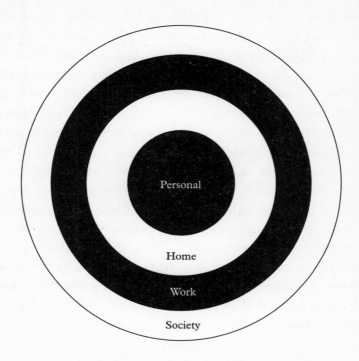

Ripple 1 – personal impact

On a personal level, there is confusion, competition and guilt – confusion about who we are and what our roles are; competition about who is more deserving of the lie-in, who should cook the meal and do the shopping; and guilt about never having enough time for our friends, family, partners, parents, children, work or hobbies. Too often, we feel in the wrong place at the wrong time.

Pulled in so many directions, it is not surprising we feel uncomfortable. But such feelings are natural. Just as the snake squirms to shed its old skin in order to adapt to its environment and feels comfortable once it's off, so, too, are we in a constant state of squirming and shedding, with our old skin hanging half-on, half-off, but the bright, fresh skin peeping out from underneath.

The rise of female equality in the workplace (or the perception of it) has had a huge impact on the home, exacerbating some core gender struggles, challenging generations of social conditioning and shaking some deeply held beliefs. I believe most of this goes on at an unconscious level, and is never openly acknowledged.

'I just want an easy life' and *'you're never satisfied'* are common arguments between men and women. They represent not problems in that relationship, but a lifelong learning of collective intelligence about the very essence of our being. Some women are never satisfied, they always want more, will always want more and right now they are getting more. Eve's scandalous eating of the apple ruined Paradise, rendered Adam destitute and Eve an outcast, yet it led to the world as we know it, a positive, amazing, extraordinary place. The message is clear – Paradise ain't enough. Women want the grit, the friction that they believe will create the pearl. They hanker after the ultimate beauty. *'Don't cosset us in too much Paradise,'* women say, *'because if it comes too easily, we'll break it to seek more.'*

Men, on the other hand, are by and large comfort-seekers. Given the choice, they will veer towards an easy life. The easy life, however, can often be mistaken for the status quo. But the easy life this time, I believe, is to be found in *not* resisting change, by *not* clinging to the status quo. It is the resistance that causes the difficulties. By being receptive to new ways, change can occur naturally and life can be easy.

Other aspects that I hear and sense of differences between genders are the different aspects or 'masks' that we stereotypically present to each other. On the outside, the man is strong and hard, his strength allows him to hunt and gather for his family, to protect and nurture them. His exterior strength surpasses that of most females. Yet at the core is a tender, vulnerable place. The female, on the other hand, soft and rounded, is weaker on the exterior but has an inner core of strength. She knows what she must do to achieve her goals. She will break the rules if she has to. From Eve's very first experience of rule-breaking, religious or not, we have been fed subliminally with the fact that, deep down, Eve is bold, a rule-breaker and always wants more than she has. The inner strength of the female, disguised by that soft exterior, is subliminally recognized by men. They see it and are drawn to it. It upholds and supports them, yet they are cautious of it as they sense their own vulnerability beside it.

In relationships, when the single man meets the single girl, the external face meets the external face. But, as the relationship gets deeper, and the internal face meets the internal face, the emphasis shifts. The internal core of the man, the vulnerable part, meets the strong, solid core of the woman and in doing so goes one of two ways. He either falls softly into that strength, relieved and relaxed to be swept up in it, or he fights it. *'This is not how it is meant to be,'* he cries. *'I am supposed to be stronger than you, to be able to love and protect you, to provide for you.'* And, as his female's core strengthens, flexes and flies higher, he becomes scared and confused. *'I am inferior, you are superior,'* he believes mistakenly, weeping on the inside as flashes of anger occur as he raises his strength in the way that millions of years of male conditioning has taught him. *'I am the boss, I am the provider, let me do my role.'* The female becomes confused. She wants to help not hurt.

It is not about one being stronger or more superior, it is about helping each other, winning together, growing together. And so the female has a choice. She either flexes her power and grows on her own, subverts her power in order to make the male feel strong again, or chooses dual growth. The female, ever interested in connectedness and relationships, will often choose the latter path. And therein lies the opportunity for growth for us all. It's a win-win situation.

Some have immediate resonance with these tensions, and others reject this debate, insulted. There's usually no in-between. Such is the heat and emotion attached to these matters. And it is oh so easy to be knocked off balance when we feel like that. The social conditioning of gender roles is deep within us. We need to re-learn together, to grow together to find new ways of inter-relating, tapping into each other's strength and weakness so that relationships are genuine collaboration and teamwork and not a competition. What we need to learn is that we can not only be strong together, we can also be weak together, and we can be strong and weak together in any combination at any given time. In our weakest moments, when we lose sight of our strength, we need the strong arms of our partners there to hold us and protect us. In our moments of greatest power, we again need the strong arms of our partners there to hold us and protect us. For our power is as fearful to us as our vulnerability. We fear our own greatness and our own vulnerability. All of us.

This inner core is being encouraged to come out into the open, to show itself more often in today's society. It does not mean a detraction of power from men or the relationship. It is 'power together' not 'power over' that will prevail. Inter-dependence, connectedness and relationship-building have long been more important than status as female values and now they are becoming cultural values too. So, as this imbalance is playing out, there is a need for support and communication in relationships more than ever. As I see it, women can let go of the need to emulate the male game, and recapture some of their femininity, articulating their gratitude to their partner or male friends or colleagues for their differences, their maleness, their contribution. And men can let go of their debilitating fear that their vulnerability will be exposed and shame them, and can collaborate rather than compete with each other and with women.

Ripple 2 – impact on home life and the changing role of parenthood

How do babies fit into these shifting power bases? Although the woman still carries the baby for nine months, gives birth, breastfeeds, nurtures and, in most cases, does more of the childcare, it is well documented that the role of the father has changed dramatically. Today's fathers attend 90 per cent of all births, a far cry from the excluded father of yesteryear. And as two-thirds of women return to work after the birth of their first child, compared with half just 15 years ago, the workload at home is expected to be shared. Again, a far cry from what happened a generation ago, when most children were brought up with relatively little input from their fathers. So what does this mean for the changing role of both parties in households with dependent children?

The new working fathers
When I first decided to write this book, the idea was centred round the issue of finding the right balance between work and family, specifically for working mums. However, as I

conducted my research, I realized that the imbalance is not just felt by working mums. Working dads are suffering too. (And, as you will see in the next section, so are those without children). They are expected to merge their roles just like women: they are expected to be able to take the child to the doctor, to attend school sports days, or to be home early twice a week to relieve the nanny. They, too, feel the pressure. How do they send out that single-minded, committed message to their employer when they're off doing the father role in its new guise? It is more hands-on than they anticipated, especially given their experience of their own fathers. Employers are torn between wanting to support family life and yet feeling that inevitable frustration when they hear that someone has dropped everything to go and pick up Jack from school. Somehow, employers will accept this more readily from a working mum but if it comes from dads it causes a strange and confusing reaction. Something I have heard from leaders (both male and female) is that they feel very torn about their male staff when they show signs of wanting to be with their family too much. They are frustrated by what they perceive as a lack of commitment, but know they shouldn't be. This makes them feel guilty and confused.

Take my client John, who had an excellent number two, Chris, whom he trusted and admired. However, he felt concerned by Chris's lack of drive and commitment because of the 'power' his wife and family had over him. *'If Chris's wife says she'd rather he didn't do something like an evening out or a trip abroad, then he won't do it. We wanted to offer him a job in our head office, but he won't take it because of her. I know it's really un-pc of me to say it, but it does limit the opportuni-*

ties of promotion.' We dealt with the situation by focusing on
Chris's strengths and Chris was duly promoted. But then
John was promoted to head office himself and Chris had a
new boss who had none of John's reticence, whose own ethos
was *'work comes before your family'.* Three months later Chris
was made redundant.

Was it just because he wouldn't travel or do evening
engagements? Probably not, but for me, it begs the question
*'Why should he be penalized (perceptually or actually) for
wanting to spend time with his family?'* The answer, of course,
is that he shouldn't, but it is an interesting case study of how
the balance is shifting so that the issues usually faced just
by working mums are now being felt by working dads. A
recent study showed that working dads report the greatest
level of stress of all executives. This is not surprising, because
as humans we are happier when we are clear about what our
role is, when we know what is expected of us and how we
can make a meaningful contribution. Once this is lost, up
pop those telltale signs of distress: loss of energy and enthusiasm, de-motivation and ultimately stress, which leads to
relationship or career plateaus or even breakdowns.

For the new father the expectations are not clear and nor
are the rules, because they are making them up as they go.
As one of my clients put it: *'It used to be so clear for my dad:
he went to work, he earned the money. It was Mum in the main
that looked after us and he would do his bit at weekends, high
days and holidays. He could be single-minded. Now, I have to
do the shop at least once a week, I have to phone Sarah* [his
wife] *in the afternoon as we negotiate who is busiest at work*
[subtext: who needs to cave in and go home early], *then
when we're at home we argue about who is the most tired. She
earns more than me so we have an unspoken battle about whose*

job is most important. While all this is going on I'm expected by my boss to be Mr Highflying, focused career man. I feel exhausted.'

Role-clarification is essential for stress-free functioning. The changing role of working dads is being acknowledged to some degree by increased paternity leave and improved family-friendly policies, all of which help. The working dad role has become more like the working mum role and the ability to multi-task, juggle and merge roles is now a required skill. It's a skill typical of the female archetype that men can now look to enhance. Acknowledging these changes rather than resisting will create an easier work–life balance.

In some cases the man finds he would actually prefer the more singular focus on work and doesn't actually want to be sharing the childcare/home roles. Some of these men become bound up in confusion and guilt, especially if their wife works too. He admires her for her career, likes the extra income and knows that he should accept the equality of his wife in the workplace but part of him hankers for a more straightforward splitting of the roles.

One of my clients laments each time his wife has returned to work after a maternity leave (they have three children): *'When she's on maternity leave she's like a different person, she's softer, more involved and it feels like she's more committed to the family. It's a wonderful feeling knowing you are going home to your wife and children who've been together all day. You are going to have a meal together and face a relaxed, home-focused wife rather than a stressed-out woman. I know it's old fashioned but it's how I feel.'*

I've also heard her side: *'I love my maternity leaves and the home definitely runs smoother, I'm happier, warmer and I know Mark much prefers me like that, but it's because it's only for a period of time that I enjoy it so much. If I was at home full time, that idyllic little scene wouldn't exist, because I want and need more than just being at home with the kids all day, as much as I love them, and I'd get resentful'.*

You can hear the conflict between the acceptance of the situation and the hankering after a more traditional split of gender roles. As Mark says, *'I love the thought of providing for my family, there's something about it that makes me feel really, really great.'*

The new working mothers

Recent years have seen a shift in the workplace as women reclaim their rights to be women and mothers as well as loyal employees. They are taking longer maternity leave, they are pushing the agenda on flexi-options, they are starting businesses and protecting their time with their families. And, perhaps the biggest shift, they are being admired, respected and emulated, not frowned upon.

They have much to thank the previous generation for. Many of those women took the 'I'll be back at my desk within two weeks' approach and, with bursting breasts and a visceral tearing of that early emotional bond between mother and baby, they returned to work and acted almost as if nothing had happened. They rarely used their children as an excuse for lateness or non-availability, because their male counter-parts didn't. They sat in meetings late, they travelled a lot, they worked harder than perhaps they felt they should, and the end result is that the 20- and 30-somethings of today who have grown up watching that generation of older successful women are questioning their approach. Is it too high a price to pay? Where's the balance? Why do you have to sacrifice your family to be a success? In fact, if you sacrifice your family life, how can you even *be* a success?

However, as this younger generation have fought to win back their birthright of motherhood and homemaker, they have refused to let go of their newly acquired seat at the boardroom table. And in refusing to pretend to be men, refusing to pretend they don't have children, and refusing to pretend that work is more important than family, they increase the feminine energy in the workplace. I believe it is the rise of the feminine spirit that is allowing women to behave in this way, that the rise of the feminine archetype is a natural rebalancing part of our development as a race. It provides an environment where more feminine values are encouraged and nurtured, so this re-assertion of femininity and motherhood and family values is being received by tender, receptive ears, not derided or ignored as it may have been in the past. They say everything has its moment, and feminine values are heading towards theirs.

However, while there are workplaces that are receptive to such change, there are still many that are not. Where feminine values are *not* accepted or admired, some women can experience a sense of extreme compromise and this new, dual-role woman – the worker-mum – sees her world fall out of balance. She wants to have a life with her children and she wants her career. If she is not supported, but feels sufficiently confident, she takes action. To correct the balance she devises a flexible working pattern or another way of working that suits her. If her company listens and can accommodate her requests, she stays, keeping her power, talent and loyalty within the company; if the company doesn't listen, or can't accommodate her, she goes, taking her power with her. She sets up her own business, she goes freelance, she consults, she invents, she re-invents, and she gets her life back in balance again. For some, this means a four-day week, for others it means full-time work, for others still it means a month's project a year. It doesn't matter how she works, what matters is that she has merged her roles, found her balance and regained her power.

For some working mums, the compromise feels untenable, yet they feel powerless to act and the struggle to achieve a work–life balance becomes the bane of their lives. But balance *is* achievable and, as I outlined in Chapter 1, it doesn't have to necessitate leaving a company or even working part-time. Finding the right balance is about regaining control and choice. The most important point, as I see it, for today's working mother is for her to recognize that her own quest for balance is entirely as it should be. It is the most natural thing in the world.

Backlash among workers with no children

As working mums and dads grapple with these issues of work–life balance, and companies begin to introduce more family-friendly working conditions, there has been a back-lash from those who choose not to, or do not yet have children. Many have their own, different set of work–life balance issues, and many also feel life spiralling out of control – often as a result of the fact that the female is now working as hard as, if not harder than, the male in the game of long hours and climbing the corporate ladder.

One of my clients, Gayle, who's in her 30s with no children, took a year off work to relax and try and conceive. Unfortunately, she and her partner had no luck and have reconciled themselves to having no children. Now back on the corporate ladder and working flat-out, Gayle hankers after the existence she enjoyed during her year off and is looking to reduce her working week to achieve more balance in her life.

With two partners working full-time the balance of a smooth, tranquil home life is hard to find. Those not in relationships hanker after balance just as legitimately as those with partners or children. They hanker after more time to pursue hobbies and see their friends, to do marathon running, or look after elderly parents, or simply achieve a better quality of life. Another of my clients was single but committed to obtaining a better work–life balance. He wanted a more varied, colourful life. He wanted more than 'just the office' in his life. Why should we wait for marriage and babies before we seek balance?

Ripple 3 – impact at work

The collaborative, softer skills, the emphasis on interpersonal relationships and facilitative leadership styles are all traits associated with the female and they represent the new leadership paradigm, replicating many of the competencies of emotional intelligence that is now widely accepted as a better way of working.

I was recently called in to coach a lady who had been promoted but had such an aggressive management style that she was feared by those around her. Eileen's style was to intimidate, bully and bark at her staff to get results. What quickly became evident was that she was working from a very outdated model of what someone in charge should do. Once we had explored alternatives and discussed the latest thinking in leadership and management theory, encouraging more coaching and empowering styles, Eileen felt a light bulb go on. She realized she could be her, be warm, be human and still gain respect. She realized she had permission to do things differently.

But the absolutely fascinating result was not so much the changes in her management style, but in her appearance. Each time I saw her, there was a visible softening of the way she looked. At our first meeting, I was aware of a very masculine persona: her hair was scraped back, her makeup was harsh, she wore trousers and heavy boots. By the end of our programme her hair was a mass of soft curls around her face, her makeup was softer, and she wore funky skirts with the heavy boots. I drew attention to the fact that her look as well as her outlook had visibly softened and she laughed in agreement, saying '*lots of people have commented on how much softer I look*', and it was having a very positive effect in the way that people were interacting with her. She was a great example of someone so in touch with her masculine energy that she'd lost sight of many aspects of her feminine energy. In focusing on some of the softer skills in her management style, it seemed to unleash a desire to re-connect or rebalance in other aspects of her life.

The rise of the feminine archetype is impacting the workplace, not only by encouraging different management styles, but also by changes in the desired working conditions. Many employees are seeking better work–life balance from their jobs. Such has been the drain on talent as people leave to find more appealing options that companies have launched large-scale work–life balance initiatives backed by the Government. Employers know they have to look after their people now or lose them. Pay rises aren't enough any more. The financial contract (as detailed by some work–life studies) is supplemented by an emotional contract. The employee now expects to feel fulfilled and cared for and supported in their life. Honouring the importance of work–life balance, historically associated with women, has become a top agenda item for companies, both big and small, male and female.

Ripple 4 – feminization of society

The rise of the feminine spirit has affected far more than just the workplace. It can be seen in design, in architecture, in the curves in the new restaurant, in the fact that the news is read by a female. It is also apparent in the ultra-feminine trends in fashion, the trend towards sweeter alcoholic drinks, multi-functional products, the use of female role models, and the open support of family and/or daughters by politicians. The list goes on and on. Feminine energy is cool, they say, it is a rising trend. I say it's one that's here to stay for some time yet.

We often feel a sense of loss when things change, but it is important to see this shift in our society as a natural self-regulating way of returning us to equilibrium. We should not resist the rise of the feminine energy, but move with the rhythm of the change as a new era creates greater harmony and greater emphasis on inter-dependence and nurturing.

SUMMARY

Society is going through a process of rebalancing as it opens up to the power of the feminine spirit encapsulated in typically feminine qualities such as nurturing, relationship-building and collaboration, and moves away from the typically masculine attributes of competitiveness, action and hierarchy. This mass shift impacts on us as individuals. As traditional gender roles are questioned, it forces us to reassess our own roles and behaviours both at home and work. It's no small task but if we are to achieve a good work–life balance we must understand where the sense of imbalance is coming from, because it is only then that we can take positive action to regain our balance. If we understand the cultural context of feelings of imbalance it allows us to be open to this change and see it as an enriching opportunity to grow and develop.

Interactive session

Rebalancing masculine and feminine energies

- Acknowledge the masculine and feminine energies within you. How do they play out at home and work? What sort of behaviours do you display?
- Ask friends or colleagues how they perceive you. Which 'energy' do they most associate you with? What would they recommend if rebalancing is required
- Consider what your balance is at home and at work. Draw a 2x2 matrix, like the one in the diagram below, with masculine energy and feminine energy in the top two columns and work and home down the side, then note what the percentage split is at each place. One female client found she was 70:30 in favour of masculine energy at both work and home.
- Now, which if any needs adjusting? My female client, for example, wanted to achieve a masculine:feminine ratio of 60:40 at work and 40:60 at home.

Current Situation

	Masculine Energy	Feminine Energy
Work	70	30
Home	70	30

Desired Situation

	Masculine Energy	Feminine Energy
Work	60	40
Home	40	60

- List some ways in which you could honour each energy to create the most appropriate balance for you – e.g. stop making *all* the decisions at home (to be less masculine), show more vulnerability at work (more feminine), dress in a softer/harder style.

Role clarification

- List three areas in which you would like more role-clarification – e.g. in your relationship, at work. When you receive this, note the positive impact it has on your sense of balance.

Rituals

- Flex your feminine energy daily – if you are male, collaborate, support, listen, nurture, express more vulnerability openly; if you are female, receive, be grateful, nurture, 'be' rather than do, express vulnerability openly – and notice what happens. Look for ways to go with the trends, not against them.
- Talk regularly to your partner about what your roles are.

WHAT . . .

can we do about improving our work–life balance?

. . . Stop making excuses

4

Reasons and Excuses

We've explored 'why' we feel out of balance, now we need some action. Now we have a context, a sense of why we are all experiencing such a strong sense of imbalance, we can get busy looking at WHAT we can do about getting more balance in our lives.

There are no *reasons* for not making desired changes in our lives, just *excuses*. We call them reasons in order to legitimize them, but in reality they're excuses. Excuses we give ourselves about why we don't change our situations, why we don't get our acts together, why we don't have more balance in our lives. When I hear clients give so-called reasons for not achieving better balance, a warning bell sounds in my head, for I know that they are not the real issue, just the symptom, the little runny nose that we focus on when a full-blown allergy is raging within the body. They are the excuses that will enable us to preserve the status quo, the safe situation that is familiar to us and that we cling on to for fear of the unfamiliar.

'I need the money. I couldn't find another job as well paid as this one. I can't work fewer hours because I couldn't get the work done. I can't take a lunch break because I'd still be here at ten o'clock at night. I can't get another job because I'm too old. I

have no transferable skills. I'm hopeless at interviews.' The list of 'reasons' is long and often extraordinarily creative. The imagination is both powerful and overpowering. When it is driven from confidence and positive energy it is a creative and empowering source of inspiration. But once in the grip of fear, our imagination renders us paralyzed, powerless in the shock of the enormity of all that could be and all that could happen in the terrifying world of the unknown.

This is what it boils down to: fear of the unknown. We are scared. But what is it we are so scared of? So much, it seems. I've heard my clients and my friends terrify themselves with the most horrendous images. They may not be scary to me as an observer, but an individual's imagination is incredibly clever, ensuring a bespoke presentation of personal fear that is guaranteed to have the individual hiding behind the metaphoric sofa of life.

The unknown and the known

The *known* is rarely scary. It can be painful, boring, stressful, draining, but at least it is known, and known equals safe. The fear of the *unknown* is well documented, yet the solution is simple: *to alleviate fear, make the unknown known.*

Many of my clients want more balance in their lives, but this requires them to do something they haven't done before. Direct action is a great thwarter of fear. Taking steps to break up the dark, cavernous space of the unknown with some shafts of light creates a sense of possibility and comfort. The unknown becomes visible, touchable and possible.

Tessa hated her job. She had been doing it for ten years, through two maternity breaks, and was 'locked in' with share options. She felt the situation had become untenable. She had been wanting to leave for over a year, yet had done little about it. But now things were bad. Her employers were cutting costs by not hiring people to replace those that left and downgrading positions by taking on inexperienced people. Tessa, as one of the old hands, was feeling the brunt of this. The morale was terrible and she longed to leave. But she said she would never be able to find anywhere where she could earn as much money and use her skills because her market was so specialized. *'There are no jobs,'* she lamented.

'Have you looked?' I asked.

'No,' she said, *'I don't know where to start.'*

'How do you know there isn't anything then?'

'I just know,' she said.

Now clearly, Tessa didn't *know* that there were no jobs, but she *believed* it to be true, in the same way that she *knew* that the unknown is scary and the known is safe. We discussed the concept of action and she agreed to phone head-hunters and talk through her brief. The positive energy she felt from doing something to help herself engaged her in phoning many of her contacts. Within a month she had two job offers. Previously, she had let the unknown scare her into submissiveness, but action gave her knowledge, light and power.

Achievements, excuses and fear

There is a way through the apparent impasse that creates momentum to change. It enables us to achieve the balance we desire. The first thing to do is to write down – and it's essential, actually, to get this down in black and white – the so-called 'reasons' why we seem unable to achieve balance. Then we have a working list of 'excuses', for, as I said earlier, that is all they are. Now, looking at the list of excuses, we must try and think of a way round each one, a way to knock each one down. In most cases, this is surprisingly easy, but there are often one or two excuses we feel are so insurmountable that we may even start kidding ourselves that they are valid reasons. If that happens, it's a case of welcome to Excuse-land. This is a land laden with excuses and it is mutually exclusive to Achievement-land, a land of fecund opportunity and success. We cannot be in both places at the same time. It's our choice, but we can't have it both ways.

If we find ourselves in Excuse-land, it's time to take another journey, this time to Fear-land. Imagine Excuse-land built on top of Fear-land, like cities that have been built one on top of the other over the ages, burying the original city and heritage. In Fear-land, there is the legacy of fear that is our personal history and on which our excuses are based. If we are willing to look below – and yes, there are some dank and smelly remains – we can find the glory of our lost ancestry, we can find *answers*.

Let me give you an example of excuses and fears and how they are linked. One client of mine wanted another job. She acknowledged that she was a workaholic, but she wanted to find another career that was more relaxing. The 'reason' she gave herself for staying put was that no other job would pay as much and that she needed to earn that amount of money. We were most definitely in Excuse-land. Had she been in Achievement-land, she'd have found a new job or career. So, digging below Excuse-land, we connected to Fear-land. What we found was something quite astonishing and nothing to do with money at all. She felt the need to be a workaholic because it meant she didn't have to spend too much time with her daughter. She adored her daughter, but felt that if she spent more time with her, she would be unhappy. Deep down, she felt unlovable. She believed that she needed the stimulation, the praise and the 'love' of her colleagues, peers and subordinates to prove she was a success and therefore 'lovable'.

Another client wanted a promotion that was eluding him. He felt it would give him a sense of payback for all his hard work. This, coupled with the increase in salary, would justify the long working hours, both to himself and his family. The 'reasons' he gave for not having been promoted were that he didn't want to sell himself internally, that another outside candidate would be better than him, and that the ultimate decision-maker didn't know him very well. So I said to him: *'If you sold yourself internally, if you were better than the outside candidate and if the ultimate decision-maker knew you, would you have the job?'* 'Uh, no,' he said.

Off from Excuse-land and down to Fear-land we went. My client was fearful of his own success. He had been a child prodigy, intelligent, great at sports, artistic, head boy, handsome – but with every success, his popularity had decreased. In an attempt to equalize his performance and thereby win friendship, he had downplayed his talents all his life. The opportunity to be promoted into the top position running a whole European region struck fear right to his core. *'If I am too successful I will be unpopular,'* was his rationale. *'Best to be mid-range and liked.'* That's different, very different.

So when we are dealing with our so-called reasons, let us get them out and take a long hard look at them. If we can knock them down and reach our desired result, we are home and dry, we are in Achievement-land. If we can't, we are in Excuse-land.

We have a choice. We can stay in Excuse-land and wallow in our excuses, or we can dig below and confront the real, valid reason for our block – fear. Then we can work out if that fear is appropriate now, at this stage in our lives, for fear always comes from our past and is projected into the future. Who we are today is not who we were yesterday and certainly not who we were 20 years ago when the fear may have first taken grip.

Reasons and excuses. They explain why, when we *want* to do something and when we know *what* we should do to achieve it, we still cannot do it. We've all experienced this. We know we should lose weight, exercise more, drink less, work differently, be kinder, take control more – but we don't do it. And the reason we don't do it is that we are living under the illusion that our reasons are valid. They are not. Remember, they are excuses, and in Excuse-land, an excuse never exists on its own, it has an umbilical cord linking it to the heart and soul of what lies beneath the surface: Fear-land.

If we can understand this, and be brave in our explorations, then we can start to turn the *I shoulds* and *I oughts* into the more positive *I choose, I will, I am.*

Facing our fears

Our fears are thoughts from our past, and can be processed positively. We are in charge of them, but only so long as we are conscious of them. The key is not to let them sabotage us by becoming submerged in our unconscious. If we can distil our fears, if we can articulate them, hear them, see them, we can deal with them. Many of us, however, are too fearful even to have a look. We can become so caught up in the here and now, and by who we want to be that we forget to look at what might be causing some of our delaying tactics. The fears from our past need to be looked at with an adult mind.

'What if I dig up something terrible? I don't want to go digging down there. It's like a night-time scuba dive into the deep dark sea and I may get bubbles in my head and get the bends.' We are fearful of fear. Or, more accurately, we are fearful of our own fear.

The facing of our fears should be a gentle, caring affair, done only when we feel absolutely ready. We fear we may not like ourselves, that we may be ugly and emotionally scarred. Why would we want to open up the wound again? Because the wound never healed and it needs a fresh dressing, the soothing salve of a conscious rational, adult mind. The fear, the excavation, heals us and makes us stronger than ever before, more solid, more robust, more whole. So, if we feel we cannot knock down our excuses, there is another option: to journey to Fear-land and take a look around. But let us only do it when we are willing and ready to change our lives in the light of what we find.

The fears we have that hold us back can be conquered. Really, all emotions boil down to the two key ones: love and fear. We have become very comfortable with fear. It rules our lives and has done since birth. Our religion and schooling is often fear-based, plus the workplace has become extraordinarily fear-based; many of us are terrified of not doing the right thing and petrified of losing our jobs. There's fear, fear everywhere. In contrast, we struggle with love, particularly in a corporate sense. People think you've gone a bit soft round the edges if you start talking about communicating with love or leading through love, but love banishes fear, it is the antidote to it.

I was watching a cartoon with my daughter about a wicked countess with a magic potion. This potion, an ageing mist, instantly aged people as it touched them. She was going to threaten the world with it unless her demands were met. The good guys managed to find an antidote and a quite hilarious scene followed in which the countess kept puffing the ageing mist on to the heroes only to have one of the heroes puff the antidote back. Back and forth they went, young-old-young-old-young-old. It struck me that that's a bit like life with fear and love. Fear renders us old, decrepit, wrinkled, stooped, unable to escape. Love, the antidote, helps us be youthful, radiant, speedy, resilient, and able to take flight easily.

Is it that easy? Just think a few loving thoughts, and hey ho, off we go? No, it's actually that hard, for who on earth wants to face their fear? We prefer to think that Fear-land doesn't exist, but many of us have learned that it does. And through that learning has come the release and the delivery into achievement that we hanker after. It happens effortlessly, as if the hard bit is just acknowledging it's there. The dredging up, the excavating is the painful, scary part. Yet one thing is repeatedly reported: it is never, ever as bad as we imagine it would be. The shadow is always bigger than the monster itself.

Fear plays a role

We will never banish fear from our lives, nor should we. All living creatures are fearful of something. They say the lion, king of the jungle, trembles at the crowing of a cock, and we all know that elephants are scared of mice. We must accept the presence of fear and it is in facing our fears that we can grow and develop. Ralph Waldo Emerson, the 19th-century poet and philosopher, put it succinctly: *'Do the thing you fear and the death of fear is certain.'*

We all know how we have learnt from mistakes far more effectively than from advice. A good scare is often the start of a mini-revolution in our lives: the heart attack that creates a chance to nurture and support the body rather than abuse it; the embarrassment of being shown up in a meeting by not knowing our stuff ensures a rigorous and thorough knowledge of what we need to know; losing a loved one makes us re-evaluate our lives. Fear is a great heralder of change. But can we accept it rather than block it?

Let me give you an example of a client who had blocked fear to the detriment of her own health and wellbeing. Anna wanted more balance in her life. Her job dominated her life. She was on call 24 hours a day, seven days a week, and it was impacting on her relationship with her partner, her health, and her sleep (she was an insomniac). When I asked what her 'reasons' were for not having more balance, this was her response: *'I can't do fewer hours because I wouldn't be able to do my job and I'd be fired. I can't say no to the unreasonable requests because I would be fired. I can't leave this job, because I need the money.'* She had no dependants, but a lifestyle and a mortgage to maintain.

I flipped the situation. *'So if you did say no more often, did fewer hours or left this job, would you have more balance in your life?'* *'Yes,'* she said. So we looked at knocking down each excuse. We looked at assertiveness to help her say no, we looked at time-management, alternative career options. No joy. We needed to go to Fear-land because these excuses were just symptoms. Anna, it emerged, had a debilitating fear of failing. If she left this job, she was failing; if she worked less, she would fail; if she said no to people she was failing them; if she was fired or made redundant, she had failed.

So, do you think this woman was ever going to get more balance in her life, a better night's sleep, a better relationship, health and confidence if she didn't take a long hard look at her fears? Not a chance. She had to stop blocking them. Fortunately, Anna was desperate for change and willing to take a look at her fears. We found that they stemmed from her childhood when she had an inordinate desire to please and never to fail. She knew she had to address this. Her 'failure' now was in allowing herself to be sucked into a life that was damaging to her health, her confidence and relationships. She realized that she needed to look again at her definitions of failure and success.

In order to help her overcome her fear of being fired, she decided to research alternative career paths, to look at her finances and take proactive steps towards achieving a life that wasn't a failure. In redefining her understanding of what constituted success and failure with adult maturity, she realized that failure at this stage was a failed relationship, poor health and low self-confidence. Success was health, happiness, a fulfilled relationship and a blossoming career. She now looked at her current job in the context of a failed life – which would be the end result if she stayed in this rut – rather than life through the eyes of a failed job. She knew then that changes needed to be made and, more importantly, *could* be made.

Anna took voluntary redundancy six months later. She was already a long way down the track in establishing another career and had six months' money in the bank before she accepted the company's redundancy cheque. She exited with grace rather than feeling humiliated. Within a month she was in a new job that was less stressful and more creative. It paid the same salary. She was on her way to being a success according to her new definition. Her fear of failure, in the cold light of day, had actually galvanized her into action. The very thing Anna thought would be a failure was the very thing that became her success.

Parallel pathing

I believe there is an easy approach that defies our paralyzing excuses and fears and it is to do with action. Taking action diffuses fear. It puts us back in the driving seat, makes us feel in control. More importantly it gives us this all-important sense of having a choice. I call this successful strategy that combats fear 'parallel pathing'.

Parallel pathing is a means of looking at other aspects of our life at the same time as living another. Many people 'play' their lives following the mantra of '*When I . . . then I . .*' It goes like this: when I earn X then I'll do Y; when I've done enough good things at work, then I'll get my bosses to define my role and status; when I retire, then I'll be happy; when I've worked flat-out for five years, then I'll enjoy my children. Whoops, there life goes, passing us by. Life does not need to be linear. Some people appear to have happiness on hold: *I'll work hard now (with no real sense of happiness), so I can retire early.*

Carl was like this until one day he woke up, aged 40, and realized his babies were strapping boys of ten and eight and his marriage was on the rocks. He and his wife split for a while as he tried to sort out his priorities. He realized he'd been crazy to work so hard and neglect his family. He went home, the family are now back together, and he has taken on assistants. He now never works weekends and takes regular holidays with his family. Happiness and family life can run alongside a job.

We do not have to wait for the 'when' to deliver our desirable 'then'. We can start the 'then' by taking tiny steps towards it now. If we are interested in becoming an interior designer, a screenwriter, a teacher, we must start researching that career option *now*. If we think our position is under threat, we must start to explore our options *now*. Action beats fear. Take the initiative. Don't wait for life to chew us up and spit us out. We must be ready for action now.

The key is to consider two things: what is our fear and what is our desire? We are looking at where we are coming from (the fear) and where we are going to (the desire) and instead of staying stuck in the fear, we are looking for ways to work alongside the fear before we are ready to break free of its hold completely. Parallel pathing gives us a way of doing that. It is a series of small but constructive actions that we take from our existing position but which lead us to a new life. If we find we don't like what we are discovering along that parallel path, it is easy to remain on the one we already know. As we tread our parallel paths, we become braver and more confident because the stepping out along this path brings with it knowledge of the world out there, the world that is slightly different from the one we are in at the moment. As it becomes known, it becomes less scary.

Simon is an excellent example of someone parallel pathing. Simon had been a senior executive in an advertising company for many years, but had decided he wanted to do something that incorporated travel and languages. He negotiated a new contract with his employers that kept him in a senior role but was more project-based and gave him three months off a year to travel, attend courses and work on developing new skills. Had the employer said no to his proposal, Simon would have left the company. As it happens, he is still running these parallel paths some three years on, and he is thoroughly enjoying the balance it provides.

Other people take evening classes, build contacts, read around a new subject or do voluntary work. This all helps keep us fulfilled because, ultimately, the benefit of a parallel path is that we won't wake up one morning and face our biggest fear: that we are insignificant and our life has no meaning. Parallel pathing takes us closer to the deeper, rounder lives that we are all searching for. My advice is to start early. Don't wait for the fear to take such a grip that you are powerless to move. The deepening of our lives need not be age-related or life stage-related. It can happen as early as we like if we choose to be proactive. And in taking these parallel paths we always have a sense of choice, a great banisher of fear.

SUMMARY

Many of us lack balance in our lives *not* because of the hours we work or the stressful job we have or the relent-less pace of the rat-race, but because we are too fearful to make the changes that would take us to a balanced life. Sometimes, as a coach, all I need to do is point this out to people and they do the rest themselves. It's as if by giving ourselves permission to know that our reasons are a sham we can stop listening to them, stop clinging to them and stop trotting them out. Instead, we can cut to the chase, if we choose to.

Interactive session

Tackle your excuses and fears

- List all the reasons you believe to be at the root of your imbalance. Welcome to Excuse-land!
- Then knock them down, one by one, to find your way through to achievement.

Or, if you can't knock the excuses down, tackle the underlying fear in the following way

- Examine what fear these excuses are linked to. Welcome to Fear-land! Once we understand our fear there is usually a rush of energy or relief because if we know what's wrong, we can do something about it. It's a case of conscious incompetence.
- Then examine the fear in the cold light of day to see where it came from, how valid it is now, and how to tackle it. Often, it is at this point that we realize we *can* overcome it, for it is a fear that started small and has become magnified over the years by never being given a voice. The silent fear is greater in every way

than a voiced fear as it cannot be faced with the maturity of an adult mind.

Take positive steps towards your goal

- Follow the steps above, having in mind the goal you would like to achieve.
- Think of a situation in your life in which you are accepting the status quo because the unknown seems too big, daunting or scary to tackle.
- Now list three small actions that you could undertake to make the unknown more known. It could be as simple as calling a friend, checking something on the Web or sending off for some information. Notice how much better you feel after having taken some positive action.

Live now

- List all your *'when I . . . then I'* tendencies. If you can't think of any, ask a colleague, partner, friend or family member. They'll know.
- Now come up with two or three definite actions that could take you on a parallel path. Don't wait, do it now!
- Make them happen. Don't forget: action gets results!

Rituals

- Ask yourself regularly, when you are stalling, what am I most afraid of?
- Parallel path – take actions to create the life you want alongside the life you have.

HOW . . .
can we get more balance
in our lives?

. . . Our band of balance

5

Our Personal Band
of Balance

There is a place out there, a place of balance waiting to be claimed by us. We do not have to live life at breakneck speed, at a relentless pace, if we don't want to. We know by now that we all have choices about how we live our lives, choices about how we plan our diaries and choices about how we react to situations at every moment of every day. We may choose to ignore these choices, preferring to believe that they are not genuinely there, that the concept of choice floats just beyond our reach. But the decision to not-believe is a choice too.

But there is a life of balance that belongs to us and only us and is ours for the taking . . . if we want it. It is waiting in the wings until we cry: *'Enough is enough. I can't, won't or don't want to carry on like this any more.'* When we decide to face our fears, decide to embrace the changes that are inevitable, when we reach out for more, that's when we can open our arms, hearts and minds to a life of balance.

And the good news is that we need not look far for it. Balance is within us. It is often described as a place, a zone, or a band, and if we stay within the boundaries of our band, we are in balance. If something tips us out, so that we are operating either side of the band, we are out of balance and we need to do something to get us back in. Too much work tips us out. Too little tips us out. All sorts of things can contribute to us being outside our balance zones, but what is important is that when we are in it all is well. We are balanced.

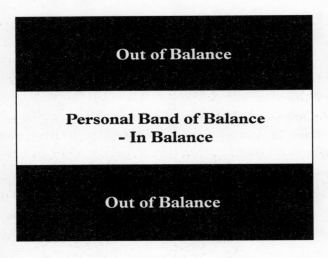

I call it the Personal Band of Balance or PBB. It is the place that we find ourselves in when we know we are in the right place at the right time, when our head isn't brimming full of should dos and must dos. Our minds are quiet and supportive of the choices we are currently making. There are three central tenets to the PBB. Firstly, it is personal, unique and peerless; secondly, it is an inner balance, it is about an internal experience rather than absolutes; thirdly, it is a dynamic balance, never exactly the same twice but changing constantly, as we, as humans, do. Gaining more balance in our lives requires us to trust that we *can* achieve it. I believe, at any given moment of time, we *can* get more balance in our lives, immediately.

The first tenet – it's personal

Our Personal Band of Balance is unique. Acknowledging that our idea of balance is ours and ours alone sounds absurdly simplistic, but needs to be said. It may be similar to somebody else's but it can't be or won't be the same because we are we and nobody else is.

Why are we often found searching for balance in somebody else's backyard? Enjoying more balance in our life is achievable but it is something that is not bought off the shelf. A three-day week offers no balance at all for some personality types. Some of us are more balanced working full-time than those working a two-day week. If I am a worrier, leaving work at 6 pm every night might cause me greater stress, anxiety and imbalance than if I stayed to finish my work.

Take Paul, he works full time, frequently entertaining clients two or three nights a week. Often he will go home, read the children a story, have dinner, then start work again at home, staying up until the wee hours. That sounds out of balance to many, but not to Paul, who knows he would feel more out of balance if he didn't work that hard. It would stress him out more if he didn't complete the work. Paul is a doer and a self-confessed workaholic. He's making a choice and it is with great pride he tells me that nothing can encroach on his weekends or holidays. That's Paul's band of balance.

For many of us we would feel overwhelmed by such a schedule, but not Paul.

Anya is at the other end of the spectrum. She works one day in fourteen, and if she feels the workload gets too stressful she feels out of balance. Pah, someone like Paul might say, but our band of balance is highly personal, and cannot be governed by what others think. The key to the problem is that most of us haven't taken the time to think about what our own band of balance looks like. What do we actually want from balancing work and life commitments? What is our ideal?

Rachel was terrified of her second marriage breaking up for the same reason as her first. In her first marriage she had got the work–life balance totally wrong and her drive and ambition meant she lost touch with her husband and the relationship broke down. To her it was essential it didn't happen again. She worked full time and her husband looked after the children. She had to find a way to stay in balance. When we really questioned what would be her ideal balance, it transpired that it was only a few more hours a week that she wanted. Her emphasis was much more about getting work 'right' so she headed home calm and relaxed able to respond fully to her husband and children. Rachel's response epitomizes many people's response to work–life balance.

For these people, work–life balance is not about working fewer hours. We don't necessarily want more time away from work, we just want to feel productive and good about it, because that frenzied, distracted or exhausted shell that heads home does not feel as if it belongs to someone leading a life that's in balance. That same person can work the same hours, but if they sense there is a purpose and meaning to what they do, they bounce out of the office off to their home life, feeling energized by work, not drained by it.

We all know what more balance should look like in our life, so we must stay focused on our own situation and not try to live anybody else's life. Balance is personal. We mustn't let anyone convince us it can be found in policies or formulaic responses. Such things may help, but they're not the whole answer. We have different triggers that throw us in and out of balance. The first step in understanding the 'personal' part of the PBB is something I don't often advocate, but here it is. Forget about everybody else just for a moment, go solo, be totally self-centred and self-aware and ask yourself the following questions:

*What makes **me** feel in balance?*
Immediately, 'others' will come rushing back into the picture. Typically, a sense of balance involves more positive interactions with the 'significant others' in our lives. Take Christine, for example, who has a high-flying career running her own business and who works a three- or four-day week, depending on demand. '*I know I am in balance when I can actually spend two or three hours with my daughter in a park doing nothing but focusing on her and not thinking "please hurry up" all the time. I have a sense of focusing on her and that it doesn't matter what happens after or before. That's like heaven for me.*'

The self-centredness refers to the ability to think about what balance feels like for us, and only us. It is not about factoring people out of our life. It is quite the reverse. Get focused on the personal and unique nature of our own place of balance. Forget about shorter working weeks or what someone else supposedly in control does, forget leaving the office at 6 pm. Work–life balance is not necessarily about any of those things, instead it's about how a balanced life looks, sounds and feels like *to us and to us alone.*

Most of us don't stop to consider that. We are convinced we are out of balance, we may even be convinced we have little idea what *in balance* feels like. However, for us to know what being *out of balance* feels like, means we must have, somewhere in that wonderful brain of ours, a concept, understanding or an experience of what being *in balance* is like. Otherwise, we wouldn't know that we weren't there.

One of the questions best able to stop people in their tracks when they are bemoaning their lack of balance, is to ask *'How do you know?'* *'What?'* they say, stunned into a moment's silence of confusion and incomprehension. *'How do you know you're not in balance?'* I clarify. A knowing smile often follows as they describe what balance would be like if they were in it. *'Well, when I'm balanced, I'm calmer, I talk slower, I have time for everybody and everything, instead of this, where I have time for nobody and nothing,'* as Christine, talking rapidly, told me.

We know more than we think we do about balance, and, more importantly, our own Personal Band of Balance. The journey of rediscovery begins with a shift in focus. When we think consciously about our place of balance, it sets our brain working in that direction. We get, in life, what we focus on. If we focus on our imbalance, we exacerbate the situation and we end up more out of balance than ever. Conversely, if we shift our attention to balance, which is what we actually want more of, we get different, more positive results. Our first port of call in our journey to more balanced lives is to analyze and visualize what is in our own Personal Band of Balance.

When I ask somebody *'What does balance look, sound and feel like?'*, invariably I witness the following response: a moment's internal reflection and then a voice shift into a dreamier, happier quality as the person describes their life in balance. I have yet to find anybody who was unable to answer, extremely clearly and surprisingly swiftly, after that initial moment of reflection. We all know what balance looks, sounds and feels like . . . as soon as we focus on it. Typically, people give a response that lists their activities and emotions, everyday events they would be doing or not doing, and how they'd be feeling or not feeling, but each 'list' is different. There is no one-size-fits-all answer to work–life balance. Assuming that the answer is a uniform solution, to my mind, misses the point. The road to greater balance in our lives is a personal one.

Balance criteria

Once we have a list or an understanding of what a balanced life looks or feels like for us, we have what I call Balance Criteria. These are the actions, behaviours and feelings that sum us up at times of balance. It is important to know these. The more we focus on them, the more likely we are to have them in our lives more often. Some examples from my interviews look like this:

I feel calm.
I am not rushing.
I am not writing lists everywhere.
My head isn't full of things I want to do.
I can take my children to school.
I have time to have a coffee and a croissant in a café and plan my day and my week ahead.
I can sleep more easily.
I have a strong sense of wellbeing.

I feel exhilarated.
I feel inspired.
I have ups and downs but I feel in control.

These are some of the balance criteria derived from interviews with executives, both male and female, with and without children. Notice not only the themes but the differences too: from calm to exhilaration, from cafés to school runs, from list making to inspiration. In spite of the variety of responses, there is a common factor. Their knowing what balance feels like and their clarity about what throws them out of balance serves as a pleasant surprise. Most precious, and even more surprising to them, is their instinctive knowledge about how to get themselves back in balance – but more of that later.

In order to get our lives in balance, we need to visualize what our own place of balance would look like, and then, once the path there has been uncovered, we need to take our first steps along it. And as that lovely, often-quoted Chinese proverb says: a journey of a thousand miles must begin with a single step.

Just in case any feeling of mystery around the unique nature of the PBB remains, let me dispel any concerns with a concrete example, that of one of my clients, Dan, who clarified his own first steps in order to get more balance in his life. His case highlights how one person's solution would not be right for everybody and demonstrates how easy it can be to take some small steps along a familiar but forgotten path.

Dan was doing very well. He had turned around a company that he described as 'bedlam' when he joined a year previously, and the staff were now happy, motivated and achieving a 25 per cent increase in revenue in a declining market. It was a spectacular success. But there was one problem. Dan was exhausted and close to burnout. He was sick of the relentless pace and wanted more balance in his life. If he couldn't get it, he felt his days were numbered with this company. Dan had a fiancée but, as yet, no children. For him, it wasn't the number of days or even the hours he worked that was getting him down, it was the way he was handling his time when he was at the office. It left him feeling guilty and exhausted, and he spent too much time worrying about work once he had left the office.

When we visualized and explored what balance looked like for Dan, it was the absence of piles of papers on his desk, and the lack of a backlog of work. Balance was one clear, concise, focused to-do list, rather than three or four that kept popping up in different formats, such as Post-It notes, PC lists, day-book lists, white-wall lists and so on. It also meant the ability to have some personal, closed-door time as well as group meeting time. Work–life balance meant a clear head, not 'angsting' about all that had to be done at the weekend when he wanted to be having a stress-free time with his fiancée. It might mean the same long hours, but it was time handled differently.

The backlogs were caused because meetings were being scheduled in a way that did not play to Dan's personality and working style. He was having meetings with half an hour or so between them, supposedly in order to prepare, but he was finding himself whiling away that time, unable to get really stuck into anything and then leaving the office feeling guilty and out of balance. He is a man who needs oodles of space before he can consider starting any backlog/thinking time/project work. His breakthrough moment was when he realized that he needed at least three hours thinking time before he could embark on anything meaningful. He hadn't realized what was causing the problems, and he was delighted to have unearthed the issue. Was this new to him? No. Had he 'forgotten' it? Yes. Hello again, forgotten path. By scheduling all his meetings virtually back-to-back on certain days and leaving chunks of three hours free on other days he was able to clear his backlog and work proactively on projects. The first small steps were taken.

The clearing of the backlog had a double whammy effect, which released a lot of guilt and 'headspace'. With his newly clear head, he felt in balance and his productivity and effectiveness increased with what, to him, felt like half the effort. The small steps broke into a run as his PBB came back into sight. He was a man back in balance. His new diary management helped him get rid of his headspace niggles. The near burnt-out Dan was promoted three months later to the executive board and felt great that he was on top of everything. He was still working the same hours, but using his time differently. He worked *with* time not against it to achieve balance.

The journey to a life of balance is easy enough. We must discover or remember what being in balance is like for us, and us alone. We must focus on ourselves, then uncover the path and head down it, tentatively at first if need be, until our increasing confidence has us striding out purposefully towards a happier more balanced place . . . our life in balance.

Headspace

I have come across the issue of 'headspace' often enough to believe that it is the worst type of offender. I see it as the most insidious and prolific of weeds that disguises and conceals the pathway to our place of balance. What do I mean by headspace? In itself, headspace isn't a bad thing – when it means the space in one's head, it can be very positive – but here I am referring to *negative* headspace. The sort that begins as a niggle and grows into a disproportionate sense of anxiety, often resulting in mental impotence and malaise. It ends up proving to that part of us that is looking for us to be hopeless, to fail, to disappoint ourselves that we were right all along. We're out of control.

Last year, we had a weed in our garden that I believed to be an attractive flower. It grew quickly and I, being quite fond of that slightly wild, country cottage look, rather enjoyed its tangled, teeming abundance. My mother, a keen gardener, came to stay. In one horrified look around the garden, she cursed this weed, animatedly tearing at its spiralling stems, showing me how it had wrapped itself round all our other plants and flowers and was slowly strangling them to death. Leave it any longer, she warned darkly, and all your roses and beautiful flowers will die. Those weeds are wicked, and they never stop. They will strangle everything. Well, to me, headspace is like that weed. Left to its own devices, it spreads into every nook and cranny of our minds, wrapping itself around any beautiful thoughts, strangling our creativity.

I have developed a theory about this that I call the Law of Disproportionate Headspace. It works like this: if a task takes 15 minutes to do and is put off, the 'headspace' it takes up is doubly disproportionate to the amount of time the task will take. Furthermore, that headspace will grow over time. I developed this theory a decade ago, from hearing friends complain about housework. I would respond to them like this: it is not the cleaning itself that takes up all your time, it is the anxiety and guilt and headspace that is taken up worrying about when you are going to fit it in and the fact that you're not able to relax without a niggle that takes up time. That takes twice as long as the cleaning itself. I should have had shares in a cleaning business, with the amount of people that hired a cleaner after that little speech! The point is that the 'headspace argument' strikes a chord with everyone. We all know it's true and yet we do little to combat it or take notice of it.

Positive, clear, open headspace is more important to protect than the action of the doing or the not doing because it causes more problems. Most people will claim they don't actually mind doing the few hours of cleaning, when they actually get round to it. It is the six hours of amalgamated worrying, bitching and arguing about it that causes the problems. If that's the case, pay someone to do it, because it clears out the six hours of bitching. Clearly, not everyone can afford a cleaner, although usually once priorities are sorted on creating a better work–life balance, the money can be re-directed from another area which doesn't support our well-being. It's a choice. The disproportionate sense of freedom and inner relaxation that will ensue gives rise to far better and more productive things in our lives. Now, obviously, I am not advocating that hiring a cleaner is the answer to work–life balance – I am merely using this domestic example to highlight the point.

The fact is, clearing headspace is the simplest of things to address and makes the world of difference to a life of balance. It is a case of just doing the task and getting on with it, thus preventing that familiar proverb *'a man of words and not of deeds is like a garden full of weeds'* from relating to us. Don't allow the negative headspace to grow. It is destructive, draining and disproportionately time-consuming. Clear your headspace by doing the dreaded task. Productivity, freedom and balance automatically follow. The task can never be as bad in the doing of it as what will follow if we don't do it.

In its role as chief offender, negative headspace needs to be put in its place. I highlight it now to urge us all to bring a scythe to it. It is a killer, a killer of creativity and positivity. We must cut through its dense and proliferating power. We do this by simply denying it a place to grow. Doing the task before it takes any more hold on us. Its spiralling, unsuspecting form shields us from our own sunlight. It deprives us of nourishment and ultimately denies us the opportunity to flourish in a place that is rightfully ours.

The second tenet – inner balance

It's not the things we do or the hours we work that throw us out of balance, it's how we feel about them. We have all worked until midnight on pitches or challenges, and felt in balance. Why? Because it was our choice and we felt in control.

It's about an inner balance and this is the second tenet of the PBB. Whenever we are talking about work–life balance, it is easy to assume we are talking about how many hours we work and the nature of our work there. The truth of it is we *are* talking about those things, but we are missing the crucial element. The balance or the out-of-balance comes not from those facts or events but how we experience them, how we deal with them inside our heads.

Take Katherine, who said she wanted more time with her family. When I probed further, and asked her how much more time, it transpired that she actually didn't want more time with them, just better quality time. When she gets home she's too exhausted or too distracted about work to enjoy her children or her husband. She resented, too, the fact that there was no 'me-time', as when she was at home she felt compelled to be with the family. We worked on ways to help her have more energy when she was with them. Katherine devised strategies that ranged from going into work later one day a week, so that she was able to take her children to school (at a time of day when she had a lot of energy), through to finding time to look after herself better during her working day – this included things like taking a break for lunch, improving her diet, cutting down on coffee, going to the gym twice a week, and having a massage once a month. All of these things helped generate more energy, and allowed her to work the same number of hours but more effectively and without the knock-on effect of exhaustion and resentment of no 'me-time' when she was at home.

The inner balance comes from choice. If we have *chosen* to spend long hours at work, we don't feel out of balance. Leah works a four-day week. She aims to take Wednesday off, but often has to change it. She also normally leaves work at 6 pm, but plans in advance to stay late one day a week and tells people she'll be available then. Does she feel out of balance because she doesn't always work the same days each week, or doesn't leave at 6 pm some nights and doesn't see her daughter before she goes to bed? Quite the reverse: *'I feel in control and on top of things, and because it's my choice to stay, I feel good about it.'*

The central elements of the inner nature of balance are *choice* and *control*. Take those feelings away and the feelings of balance start to go, no matter how little or how much we work. The most stressful job or the longest hours are not unbalancing if we feel we've got a choice about doing it, and we feel in control of it. So the search for more balance is not out there waiting to be handed to us on a plate, but needs to come from us getting more control and having more choice over what we do and how we do it. It's an inside-out thing, not an outside-in thing.

Companies have made terrific inroads into work–life balance. It has moved to the top of the agenda with the Government encouraging work–life balance initiatives by offering financial grants and awards. Work–life balance is being taken seriously, and if companies have invested time and money in creating policies, guidelines, charters and experimental practices, it is up to us to explore the choices offered. But remember, don't start with the choices on offer, start with our *own* sense of choice. Although it is important to work *with* employers to create the work–life balance that we want for ourselves, our employers are not mind-readers. We need to be clear in our communication about what kind of balance we want. And, for many, it will be a shift in role rather than hours. Energy comes from following our enthusiasms. Deadening comes from lack of meaning. A deadened person is not in balance and never will be.

If balance is an inner state that comes from choice and control, the next step is to shift our thinking. That shift is the internalization of the locus of control. It's about moving from victim mode to in-control mode, from *'there are no choices'* to *'I choose'*. It's about knowing that we can make things happen. That we are the buffets. That we do not have to be buffeted about by life. We cannot always control what happens to us, of course, but we can control our response. If we remain positive, if we can stay tuned into positive emotions, we will have more access to a wider repertoire of choices. And with choice and control comes balance.

The third tenet – dynamic balance

What do I mean by dynamic balance? Our PBB changes constantly, is never still. This is because life is never still. Our interchange with the world is dynamic and swirling, in constant movement. It's therefore not possible to say '*Aha, I have found my balance, over and out*', for us to put our feet up, and hope life will be in perfect balance for evermore.

When I was a young girl, growing up in the countryside, there was a place we loved to go to. We called it the weir, though it was actually a little island near the weir, and it was supposedly out of bounds. We couldn't resist it, however. It was a place of wonder and adventure to us, where we played endless games running around, crossing the river in shallow parts, swimming and building dens and fires. In fact, doing all the things that, as a parent, would horrify me now and would have horrified our parents had they known what we were up to. But the thing we loved most about the weir was that every single time we went there, it was different. Because it was surrounded by water, there were always different parts of it either hidden underwater or exposed, depending on the season. Our favourite time to go there was after a flood or a storm, to see the havoc that had been wreaked. Would the outcrop of land that allowed us to jump safely from one part of the island on to that rogue rock in the middle of the river still be there? Would the rogue rock even be there? Would we be able to have our competitions of jumping to the other side? Whatever changes nature had produced, they added to the intrigue, wonder and pleasure of the place. Yet despite the changes we always knew our way around, as if the place were our own bedroom. Some 30 years on I can still see and hear that island and the water with aching clarity in my mind. I wish I could go there now.

When I talk about dynamic balance, I am referring to the ability of life, like my childhood island, to be the same and yet wondrously, breathtakingly different with each exploration. We need not be frightened of imbalance for with it comes the opportunity to renew ourselves into something better adapted to our changing environment. When the storms and the floods come and we lose our existing shape, things can get pretty scary. But they actually leave a new shape, a new opportunity to rebalance and re-energize. When things knock us out of balance, we need not be resistant, trying to hold on to how things have always been done before. We can surrender to changes, we can allow our balance to be dynamic rather than static and we can trust that our different yet familiar place of balance will serve us better in the future.

So, the definition of a balanced life one week may not be the same the next. For me, in October, working three days a week felt fine, felt fabulous, felt perfectly balanced. In November, just four weeks later, I felt out of balance. Suddenly, three days was too much time at work. What was the reason for this? It was that in the space of one month, I felt my daughter had suddenly grown up. In that time my dependent, cuddly, adorable little girl had become confident, independent and outgoing. Of course, part of me swelled with pride at her burgeoning confidence, but part of me was crying in agony. Where had the time gone? Where had my baby gone? I can never recapture that time and I never want to look back and wish I'd spent more time with her. Our time together, with me as the centre of her world is too short and too precious. And so the simple act of shifting my working week so I can finish earlier and pick her up from school an extra day feels good right now. I feel back in balance. Will it shift again? Yes, I have no doubt about that, and when a storm comes – or in this case, what felt like a mini-drought – I'll take stock and find a way to self-renew into a better shape, a shape where the balance feels right and familiar but will be different.

Being on the outside of our Personal Band of Balance can come from under-stimulation as well as over-stimulation. Veronique was moved from a role where she ran a department of 50 people, into a roving strategic role, where she acted as an internal consultant and was based largely at home. At first, the change of pace seemed quite pleasant, then she found herself feeling out of touch, out of control and lazy. Her productivity fell, her self-esteem dropped. Her family noticed her moodiness. The lack of pace had thrown her out of balance. She addressed it, looking at what constituted her ideal sense of balance. She wanted to be part of a team, office-bound. She thrived on structure and tangible contribution and output. Two weeks later she was offered a job with another company, again heading up a department. Not only was it office-based and closer to home, it also offered a big challenge and a third more pay. She didn't hesitate in taking it. Her life, although seemingly busier and more stressful, was back in balance for her.

Tipping out of balance

When we are not in our band of balance, things don't feel so good. Noticing when we are out of balance is the first trick. It manifests itself in many different ways. It may be snapping at people in the office, falling ill or being beastly to the children over breakfast. Whatever the signs are, we must keep a look out for them. We mustn't ignore them. By listening carefully we can acknowledge that something is happening, something that has tipped the balance into a place where we are less happy. Then we must stop and take stock. Common examples of how people feel once they are outside their band of balance include:

Snapping at people
Being agitated
Getting ill
Being abrupt
Feeling sorry for themselves
Stomping around the office
Being beastly to people
Getting tunnel visioned
Obsessing about something
Forgetting things

These are known as snappish symptoms, largely because this is the trait mentioned by most people. Once we see any one or any combination of our snappish symptoms, we know we are out of balance. This is 'conscious incompetence' kicking in. We know we're doing something wrong and, as we found in Chapter 1, that's progress in itself. In the same way, we rarely take time to think about our balance criteria, those things that are there when we are in balance, and we rarely look at any of the other constituent parts of balance.

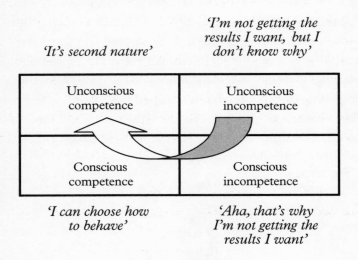

'It's second nature'   *'I'm not getting the results I want, but I don't know why'*

Unconscious competence   Unconscious incompetence

Conscious competence   Conscious incompetence

'I can choose how to behave'   *'Aha, that's why I'm not getting the results I want'*

The learning cycle

This is where the journey typically goes a bit off-piste. This is the only bit where I think the journey becomes a little tough. When we find ourselves out of balance, it plays out typically in unproductive and unhappy behaviour. We then feel bad about ourselves and start to have negative emotions. When we have negative emotions, the weed takes over, and our creative and positive responses get strangled. The technical description for this in psychology is that our thought-to-action repertoire closes down. The number of options we generate and hold open reduces dramatically.

With our options at an all-time low, we tend to carry on doing the same old things, regardless of the negative impact they are having on our lives. We lose sight of the fact we have options and we certainly lose sight of the fact that we can be more in control. This loss of resourcefulness is temporary but feels permanent. My role is to remind you that it is temporary.

In order to increase the repertoire of options available to us, we need to chop down that weed, so there is space for positive emotions, which generate more creative and numerous responses to our situation. Studies in the USA have proven the effect of positive emotions such as love, curiosity, joy and compassion on our creative response and effectiveness.

Fortunately, we are halfway there if we acknowledge we are out of balance and we want to do something about it.

Balance-tippers

It is important to analyze what tips us out of balance. Like all the other aspects of the PBB, people are always quick to respond to this one. Typical answers include:

Too much work
Someone being offhand with me
Poor relationship with boss/loved one
Being late
Not being properly prepared (for a meeting/presentation)
Too much socializing
Not enough sleep
Eating badly

Drinking too much
Mess
Disorganization
People not delivering to my expectations

Once you are aware of your three or four main balance-tippers, the key is to try and minimize the number of times they show up in your life. My clients are often amazed at this part of the process. Working out what it is that can make the difference between staying in balance and being thrown out of control, is enlightening, for while we know it subconsciously, we have probably never focused on it. The key is to crystalize the thinking and to start to establish habits that minimize the incidences of our balance being tipped. Clearly we will never live a life of perfect calm. But we can smarten up our act and start to edit the balance-tippers out of our lives.

A great example of this was Sam, who knew that 'mess' was a balance-tipper for him. He lived with a messy wife and his return home was usually greeted by chaos and mayhem, which put him into a foul mood as soon as he entered the house. He realized in our sessions the huge impact that this was having on his relationship with his family and his own sense of wellbeing. Unable to articulate it clearly before, he had just suffered the consequences of an unpleasant first hour at home, and, worse still, had started staying at the office later in the hope that when he got home his wife would have had time to tidy up once the children were in bed. He discussed it with his wife and they employed a cleaner to come to the house for two hours each day, just before he returned home. Problem solved, balance restored. The balance-tipper of 'mess' has been virtually deleted from his life and his time with his wife and children has not only increased, but more importantly, it's become more serene.

So, crystalize your balance-tippers and set about minimizing them.

Rebalancing strategies

There are times when we will go out of balance, regardless of how well we are doing on minimizing our balance-tippers. We are human and it is right and proper that we fluctuate in and out of balance, throughout the days, weeks and months of our lives. Route one to better balance is through our own rebalancing strategies, which we already have and already use. Like the path, these may be fully developed but 'forgotten', we may not be aware of them, or they may be nascent, a new path waiting to be found.

When I asked Leah about how she got back into balance, she reflected for a moment before reeling off a string of things she did. '*I tidy up, I get some fresh air and I talk it through . . . oh, and exercise – that always helps – and an early night.*'

When I talked to Mary, someone at the forefront of work–life balance issues, her way of getting back in balance was to carve out half a day and do her backlog at home, even if it ate into the time with the children, because then she was back in balance. That is a classic example of when working at a time when you are meant to be somewhere else doesn't throw you out of balance, because it's a choice. For Mary it's a *rebalancing* strategy, not an *unbalancing* one.

There are many different ways that we rebalance. The secret of success here is to ask ourselves the question in a

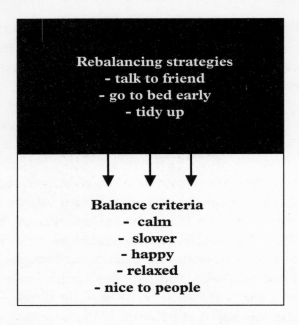

Rebalancing strategies
- talk to friend
- go to bed early
- tidy up

Balance criteria
- calm
- slower
- happy
- relaxed
- nice to people

positive way to unearth our previous successes so that we have a positive and personal case study to work from. Try this: describe a time when you made some changes, however trivial, however tiny, that helped get a situation back on track for you; describe some minor, or indeed major shifts in thinking or behaviour that got you into a calmer, more balanced frame of mind. Once you've come up with an incident when you managed to get yourself back in balance, then think through what you actually did to get there. It's like pressing the rewind button and analyzing it frame by frame. How did you get from A to B?

Take Stephen for example, a successful finance director who was young and constantly being stretched beyond his limits in terms of his knowledge. He had a deep fear of being unprepared or for 'busking' meetings, but remained successful, challenged and happy by always being on the front foot for meetings by 'over-preparing'. This he had always done during an hour or two of quiet solitary preparation time in his office, first thing in the morning. His balance changed, however, when he had a second baby and his company started working on a major acquisition project. The two events coincided to make him feel out of his depth: his rebalancing/preparation strategy was whipped away from him because he now had to take his older child to nursery. By the time he got to the office, the opportunity for quiet time at his desk, due to the natural inter-ruptions of an office in full swing, was long gone.

He was feeling out of control and out of balance when I started working with him. We uncovered the fact that he had some successful strategies that had worked in the past, which he'd 'forgotten' and/or was unable to action in his current day. By acknowledging the crucial role these strategies had played in keeping him successful he recognized firstly and importantly that he did have strategies and that he needed to find a way to update and adapt them. He started two or three small behaviour changes that got him back in balance. His thinking and preparation time happened before he came to the office, sometimes the night before at home or in a coffee shop on the way to work. He now 'knew' that having this prep time was more important for him than being seen at his desk by 9 am every morning. He also formalized the 'chasing' of people on the phone before a meeting to pin down exactly what was needed, what was expected and who'd be there. The 'not knowing' had been causing Stephen a huge amount of anxiety and unnecessary stress (headspace alert!) but by eliciting the information, Stephen swiftly achieved a feeling of control while getting the information he needed for effective preparation.

These changes helped Stephen significantly through that

period. Not only was he considered so impressive that he was put forward for a very senior promotion, but he managed to 'be there' for his wife and two children. When things shift again, he may need some different behaviours but the process will be reassuringly similar.

Acknowledging that we are out of balance, stopping, reminding ourselves of balancing strategies that worked for us in the past in related or unrelated incidents and thereby reminding ourselves of our options, widens that thought-to-action repertoire. As a bi-product, we feel more positive by remembering a time when we have been successful in gaining more balance, however transient.

Then start to put some of the easier actions into play. Success breeds success. Just the act of getting ourselves into a more proactive position of tackling what's going on is a success in itself. We move from shut-down mode, from being a victim, into someone who can make a difference. We can access our PBB more often and it can be stretched. If we rarely enter it, it will atrophy. We need to spend more time there by being very conscious. Conscious of what it looks and feels like, conscious of things that tip us into it, events and people that tip us out and conscious of what we look and feel like when we are out of balance. We've chosen to take a pathway from a life out of balance to a place where balance is just the way we like it. All it takes is a little focus.

SUMMARY

We have a band of balance when things are right for us. When we are within this band, which is very personal, all is well. When events, people or situations tip us out of balance we need to notice that we are outside our band of balance. By listening to our own snappish symptoms and being aware of our balance-tippers, we can notice and rectify the problem more quickly using our own rebalancing strategies to put us back into our band of balance. These are strategies that we know work for us at helping us gain equipoise.

Interactive session

Your badge of balance

- First draw an empty badge and divide it into four quadrants.
- Step 1: visualize your band of balance. What does it feel like when you're balanced?
- Step 2: list your balance criteria, the things that are there or not there when you feel balanced. Put this information in the top left quadrant.
- Step 3: list your balance-tippers, typical events or people that tip you out of balance. Put this in the top right quadrant.
- Step 4: list your snappish symptoms, your typical behaviour when you're out of balance. This goes in the bottom right quadrant.
- Step 5: list your rebalancing strategies, the ways you get yourself back on an even keel. Put this in the bottom left quadrant.

- The final step is to come up with a motto or slogan across the middle that will help you recognize that you *do* have a choice and that you *can* have balance whenever you want.

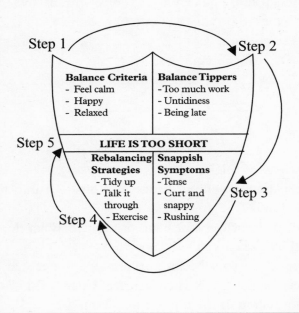

Rituals

- Minimize your balance-tippers on a daily basis.
- Create opportunities which give you more balance.
- Ask yourself daily what being in balance will mean to you *today*?
- Remember: balance is never static.

HOW . . .
to get more balance in
our lives

— *by being ourselves*

6

Permission to be Me

Imagine the journey to balance is like a fascinating expedition. We have certain mandatories, such as food, water and clothes, without which we cannot succeed. There are similar mandatories on the journey to balance and these are covered in the next three chapters. They are self-awareness, intuition and health. Without these, I believe, it is not possible to achieve a genuine work–life balance. These mandatories are ongoing strategies that we need to live and practise daily. At first, we may have to consciously remember to do them, but they soon become second nature.

James looked exhausted. *'I'm at peace at home with my family. If only I could be more myself at work, I could be more at peace here too.'* 'So when are you not yourself?' I asked. *'All the time,'* he sighed despondently. *'All the time.'*

Now James is probably an extreme case. But James will never achieve work–life balance whilst he is so busy trying to be someone else. The absolute bedrock for the journey to better balance is self-awareness and authenticity. In other words, we must know who we are and then be true to ourselves. We know this, in fact it's almost a cliché, yet it is something that troubles many of my clients, either knowingly or unknowingly. Coaching encourages us to be more of ourselves. It is not a case of radically changing. It is more a case of chiselling away at the masks and the surface pretensions to reveal our real selves inside.

We all act out of character at work sometimes, with a little posturing here, some compromising there. Many of us believe it is neither acceptable nor enough to be 'just me' at work, and often, due to a fear of being found out, we play a role, consciously or subconsciously. But when we lose sight of the essence of who we are, our sense of wellbeing and balance is affected and this is what results in that exhausted, worndown feeling. Because we spend a large proportion of our time at work, if we compromise ourselves there, we will never achieve the ultimate sense of balance that we seek. As we have learned, it is not a given that a good work–life balance will come as a direct result of shortening our hours or working week. If I am working a two-day week but feel compromised in some way by not really being me at work, I can feel more out of balance than somebody working full time who is more true to themselves in the workplace.

The way to address this imbalance, though harder in practice than in theory, is straightforward. Firstly, we need to find out who we are, then to immerse ourselves in that knowledge so we can be more ourselves. When we are true to ourselves, when we honour our values and beliefs, we experience a sense of ease and effortlessness in what we do, which results in more energy and a better sense of balance. And boy, do we become attractive. We find we attract business opportunities, relationships, creativity and opportunity. When we are more comfortable with ourselves at work, our lives naturally feel more comfortable.

I have devised a process, a cyclical one that I call the Personal Best Model, that has had tremendous success in enabling people to be more themselves, thereby giving them more authenticity and confidence in their leadership style. When I have worked with clients who have highlighted a non-specific discontent or stress at work, they are often unable to articulate the precise issue. With coaching techniques, they isolate the areas where, by not being true to themselves, they are compromising themselves. In moving the non-specific malaise to specific issues that can be addressed, they make very small changes, but achieve dramatic results. This enables them to become more self-aware, more energized, and ultimately much more effective. The main benefits at work are found in improved communication skills, persuasiveness and credibility. The internal benefits reported by my clients are improved self-confidence, wellbeing and, frankly, a huge sense of relief that it is actually OK to be themselves. This immediately creates a more balanced and positive outlook.

This Personal Best Model consists of five stages:

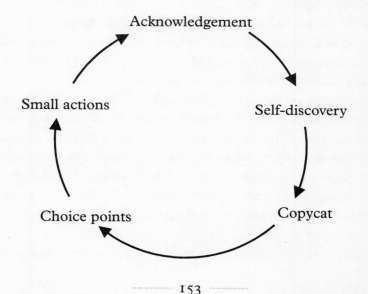

The Personal Best Model is a remarkably simple process, and achieves very positive results. Although it is probably best done with the help of a friend, colleague or personal coach, it can be done through reading and reflection too. It requires a healthy dose of honesty and self-assessment to start with, to acknowledge what is actually going on at work, where we are being ourselves and where we are not. Having done this, we move into the self-awareness stage. I have called it self-discovery because we should try and keep a sense of wonderment and discovery about what we might find. It benefits from the input of others, to ensure our self-awareness is an accurate reflection of how we are behaving or, more importantly, how we wish to be perceived by others. This stage is all about finding out *who we are when we are at our best*. Our natural modesty will often prevent us from valuing our own skills and strengths. What seems obvious and natural to us – and what we frequently take for granted – is often what others respect and admire. We can be so busy playing out a role of trying to be somebody else that we forget the value of being who we truly are.

The idea is to highlight this awareness of ourselves at our best and then copy it. This is the copycat stage. Really we are aiming to build a model of what we are like when we are confident and relaxed and at our most effective. This may sound more complex than it actually is. The 'model' is really a grand word to act as a catch-all for the different forms that this part of the process can take: a list, a graphic, a grid, or just a discussion. All we are really trying to do is put some language around what, when and how we behave when we are at our best. That way we can copy it and do it more often. It's that simple – if we focus on something, we will to get more of it.

Once we have this, the rest is about making it happen,

working out where we have choices about more positive and honest behaviour and making tweaks and small changes to become more ourselves, to be ourselves at our very best more often. As we become more true to ourselves we will feel a weight lift off us, and enjoy a newfound confidence in just being ourselves. There is nobody else like us. There can never be anyone that can think like us, who has had our experience and who will see things in the way we do, so we must harness our uniqueness and share it with the world.

Let's go through the process to see how it works in the real world.

Acknowledgement

Selling ourselves short

Juliet sat in front of me leaning forward, eyes shining, gesticulating confidently as she explained her grand vision for her marketing strategy for the coming year. We were coaching her, using a video camera, for a board presentation. I was enthused, captivated and utterly persuaded that her bold strategy would pay off. Moments later, Juliet practised it exactly as she would present it to the board. She repeated the exact same words, but this time my heart sank. The confident gestures had become nervous flapping of the hands and twitches of the face, the compelling tone was now wobbly, weedy and, bizarrely, slightly pompous. Her body language was weak.

What accounted for the sudden change? The exercise laid bare for Juliet, as she experienced the changes inside her and then witnessed them on film, the transition from being true to herself to being somebody completely different. It wasn't about nerves as she is an accomplished and experienced presenter. The problem was that she didn't believe it was good enough to be just her. She believed she needed to be more conciliatory in tone, but also have gravitas, hence the strange mixture of pomposity and weediness, never a great combination for a persuasive presentation. She was so busy being who she thought she was supposed to be that she lost her most powerful weapon – herself. When she gave herself permission to be herself, seeing firsthand how much more persuasive and powerful she was, her boardroom presence was, quite literally, transformed.

When we are more powerful than the truth

So why are we not more ourselves at work? When encouraged to think about what happens when we are being more ourselves, we unequivocally report feeling more natural, that we have more energy, are more engaged, more comfortable, more connected. And, interestingly, we report an internal feeling, a sense of 'rightness'. Try it. Ask yourself:

'*What does it feel like when I am being more me?*' (Don't worry about me-at-my-best at this point.)

The answer, usually, goes something like this: '*When I am most me, I am energized, confident, enthusiastic, engaged and engaging. I feel right.*' The benefits of feeling this way are obvious and enormous, so the question can now shift.

'*Wouldn't our organizations prefer us to be more energized, more enthusiastic, engaged rather than tired, awkward, disengaged, demotivated and, further down the line, depressed?*'

The answer is always a sheepish yet wry '*Yes*'. Of course they would. So let's get busy being ourselves instead of busy not being ourselves.

We usually have some vision in our minds as to what a leader, a salesperson, a board director (or whatever role we are focusing on) actually is. We hold up this vision as The

Truth and beat ourselves up about why we are not a carbon copy of this truth. Often, a current or former boss or an archetypal leader such as Nelson Mandela or Winston Churchill is seen to be The Truth. Either way, we cannot win. Our essence, our uniqueness will never, ever allow us to be this person, and the more we whittle away at our own self, the more we lose our power and our effectiveness.

Instead of whittling, start building. The start point is: *'Who am I? And with me being me, how do I want to handle the role?'* If honesty is an important value to you, perhaps your promotion into a new role gives you the opportunity to practise and be known for a new level of honesty. If humour is an integral part of you, then it should be part of the branding you sear on to your role. Your role becomes you, you don't become your role or, more accurately, your perception of what that role should be.

When I debate this with my clients, I notice another consistent theme. If they hold a value dear to them – let's say humour – they will ask: *'Doesn't everyone want humour in their personality, or to be known for being humorous?'* The answer is an unequivocal *'No'*. Nobody is exactly like us and just because a value or characteristic is so integral to us that we cannot imagine life without it, we must remember that no two people are the same. Even the person that we have most in common with is different in countless ways.

Typical areas of resistance

Let's take three points of resistance that typically arise. Firstly, how do I know if I'm not being me? Secondly, what if being me gets me nowhere? Thirdly, how do I find out who I am anyway?

In reverse order, who am I? Finding out who we are is a life-long journey, and is a pre-requisite of this process. It is the key to all aspects of finding balance in our work and our lives. For once we know what makes us tick, what energizes us, what drains us, we can make choices which will move us to a life of more positive and conscious choices which, ultimately, will give us the inner balance we are after. I will cover the how to find out who I am in greater detail in the next section.

Let's look at the second point of resistance: what if being me gets me nowhere? I strongly refute this. This is *not* going to happen. If we are being true to ourselves, aligned, balanced, acting with complete integrity, focusing on what we enjoy and are best at, we will go wherever we want to go. It is the 'not me' which holds us back, it is the 'not me' that gets us nowhere. The integrity of being ourselves shines through and attracts to it results that hitherto seemed unattainable.

As for the first point – how do I know if I'm not being me? – that part is easy. If we ask ourselves: *'Do I feel inexplicably and unreasonably tired none of the time, some of the time, most of the time or all of the time?'* and the answer is anything but the first option then we are compromising ourselves at some level. When we are being true to ourselves, our behaviour, interactions and decision-making are effortless and energizing. We will feel balanced, at peace with ourselves. Every time we compromise ourselves, we die a little. Our energy is drained. I don't mean making compromises with others, I mean compromising ourselves. Lying, pretending, deceiving ourselves. The sure-fire way to know is to check our energy level: if it's consistently low, check it out; if it's consistently high, all is well.

Am I being true to myself?

Give people a chance to be who they are, do what interests, excites and engages them and we see better energy, better work and a more authentic confident employee. The difference between someone being himself and giving the spiel he believes other people want to hear is unbelievably clear. The difference in a meeting or presentation between a point we've written down to remind us to mention it, and the flashes of authenticity that come through in the moments that we speak from the heart, is crystal clear. These are the points in time when we really connect with people – and we, as a human race, are obsessed with connecting with others. In many ways, it is our *raison d'être*, but we want to connect with the real person. We have an impressive, innate ability to detect when people are being dishonest on any level. We will disbelieve, or discredit something if we have the sense, from the person's tone or body language, that he or she is not speaking the truth. There is a very famous set of studies by psychologist Albert Mehrabian in his book *Silent Messages* which concludes that non-verbal communication accounts for 93 per cent of all communication. When the person is not saying the same thing in content as their tone or their body language is suggesting, the listener will believe the tone or the body language over and above the content. It is when there's a mismatch between the two that we go into a 'sensing mode' that picks up tiny little cues that we are surprisingly intuitive about. Studies consistently show how expert humans are at detecting deception. So, if there is a mismatch between how we really feel, and what we're saying, it will be spotted. Instantly.

Interestingly, it is often not picked up in any conscious way. The person we are having the mismatch conversation with senses that something is making them feel slightly uncomfortable and this is enough to register as a lack of connection, however slight, and it undermines us. Those that have absolute alignment between what they're saying, what they're thinking, what they're believing and what they do, are the people who are the most believable, are the most credible. They have authenticity. These are traits, certainly in a leader, but really in every successful human being, that are cited as what we most admire. We want to trust. We want to believe that someone who says they will deliver, delivers. Trust and credibility are consistently themes that are at the top of the list of qualities most respected in leaders.

So being 'not me' costs us too much. It costs us energy and it costs us a lack of connection that undermines our credibility. Behaving in a way that is consistently against how the real me wants to operate or believes it should operate, can cause a considerable amount of stress. We may feel a level of discomfort, discontent and unhappiness with our life, but we won't necessarily know why. We will never be truly balanced if the 'not me' outweighs the 'me' at work.

Honesty is called for at this point. The six-million dollar question: *'How am I managing in the balancing act of the me and the not me?'*

Self-discovery

Self-awareness

The first part of the strategy is to know who we are. Psychological studies published in the many journals of psychology, social sciences and occupational therapy have proved the correlation between self-awareness and wellbeing, identifying the link between positive introspection and personal development. That is to say, looking inside and analyzing who you are with a *positive outlook* (understanding your strengths and weaknesses) improves happiness and psychological wellbeing. The key is to identify our drivers, our core values, our motivators and needs, then to honour them and communicate them and brand and market yourself with complete integrity and authenticity.

Most people believe they know themselves well, and of course they do. But they know themselves in an amorphous, intangible way, in the same way that we know what the essential outline of our country is, but we don't know all the inlets, all the territory, in any intimate way. In conforming at school, through college or university and through the workplace we sometimes lose sight of who we are, so busy are we playing out the role that is expected of us. Even those of us who know ourselves well can always uncover more, and by exploring ourselves through our own eyes and through the eyes of others we can start to understand our true selves better.

How do we achieve this?

Dialogue is a crucial part of the discovery process. Even those who choose to reflect rather than talk, will need input from others as they make true discoveries through internal dialogue. The key strategy for improved self-awareness is to keep in a continual feedback loop. The best leaders constantly seek honest feedback about their performance so they can continue to improve. Top athletes and sports teams watch video footage after a match to see where they performed well or where they could have done better. They then use their coach to focus on the areas that need improving. They know that winning comes from small increases in effectiveness and efficiency. Little wins can make all the difference.

It can be extremely tough, but we need to be open and

receptive to learning about ourselves. Surprisingly, it can be just as hard for some to hear positive feedback as it is for others to hear the negatives. Discussions with friends or colleagues can work just as well. Some people prefer exercise or meditation or reading as a process to work towards self-awareness. What matters is to spend some time on positive introspection.

Exercises translated from marketing models can be very useful. For example, those that involve asking others what they *first* think of when they think of us, and what they most associate with us. The important point in this phase is that, while we are finding out about ourselves warts and all, we should be doing so in a *positive* context. The aim is to determine us at our best, when we are at our most engaged, most energized, when we achieve our best results, when everything flows effortlessly. Of course, there are times when we will be angry, stressed, obnoxious, and behave appallingly, and will also be 100 per cent you but, while it is important to acknowledge the negatives, they are not the part of us that we want to copy here.

Flexing

The Personal Best Model is about finding out about us at our best. The most frequent question I get asked when working with this model is this: *'But what about those characteristics that are required for me to be a success in my job, but that just aren't me?'* For example, take my client Bill's response, *'I am a conceptual, big-picture person and am at my happiest when brainstorming or starting an idea. I don't like detail, structure or follow-through. But if I let that run rampant, I would never finish anything and my reputation would be tarnished. How does this fit into the Personal Best Model?'*

My answer is always the same. '*It's all in the flexing.*' We have learned to adapt behaviours to gain acceptance by society and the success that we desire. Many people would claim that it's gone too far and we've lost sight of our natural selves. Having seen the raw nature of children before they've learned the social graces of sharing and manners, I argue that this is no bad thing, but we do need to learn how to flex behaviours that get us the results that we need *at the appropriate times*. In the same way we flex a muscle when we need it.

I flex my arm muscles when I pick my children up, and I stick my hip out to perch them upon it. If I walked round like that when I wasn't carrying my children, I would develop an appalling posture that would ultimately misalign my true shape, and cause considerable stress on my body and on my other muscles. This is exactly the case with our personality. We must flex the behaviours we need, as and when we need them. If they are behaviours that come harder to us and take more energy, then all the more reason to flex them only at the appropriate times. You do not need to become these behaviours – just to flex them . . . and then return to your natural position.

So, taking Bill's case, it is effortless for him to think in a big-picture way, and detail or follow-through take more energy and are less enjoyable. But he is capable of performing the skills necessary to carry out these tasks. In fact, when he puts his mind to it, he is highly competent, because he has learned the skills are a pre-requisite for success in his career. He has also learned to do the tough parts at times that suit him, remaining aware that they take effort and energy. If he had to work in a structured, detail-oriented role, working on projects that required consistent follow-through over a sustained period, he would be chronically stressed. The parts of our personality that take more energy – but which are needed to achieve the results we desire – need to be flexed *at the appropriate times,* but not all the time.

When we embark on our Sherlock Holmes career of understanding ourselves more, be aware that this is a journey that lasts, quite literally, a lifetime. The psychologist Carl Jung believed that the healthy development of our personality depends upon us uncovering and flexing parts of us in the second half of our life, which, until that point, have been under-used. For example, if I have been a person always planning my future, someone who is a dreamer, never quite in the here-and-now, I may, in the second phase of my life, develop an interest and ability to be very focused on the present and highly observant about what is going on around me. Noticing that we are starting to get pleasure from things that have hitherto bored us, or been difficult for us, starts us off again uncovering new details about ourselves. And so the investigation of self-awareness goes on. There are many tools and techniques to help with our investigation dotted throughout this book, but, essentially, any self-development work or reading will help you on this mission.

The key to success here is to know that flexing is a conscious choice. We should nurture a mature, compassionate, loving acceptance of ourselves. We need to know when to flex the different styles that are less of a reflection of our personality, but also to understand that we are flexing them for a reason, and that it will not undermine or attack who we are at our core. We flex from our core and we return to our core.

Copycat

Stephanie was desperate. She had been in her new job for six months and was convinced she was failing. She felt she had no idea what was expected from her and as a result was depressed and exhausted. Indeed, Stephanie was so desperate, she had made up her mind to resign if she couldn't resolve it. She had no idea if her boss rated her or would be pleased if she left the company. I knew for a fact that her boss thought highly of her. She was a prized senior hiring and her boss would have been devastated to think she was unhappy or frustrated. But my views were meaningless to Stephanie at this stage. She needed something else.

When we worked on her model, she realized that she had a need that wasn't being met. Stephanie needed structure and guidelines. When she had these she was at her best, highly focused, productive and effective; without them she fell into a spiral of self-pity and suffered an extreme loss of confidence. Once she had formulated her model, she was clear about what had to be done. She knew it was imperative to express her style and needs in order to become more effective and avoid an inappropriate and premature resignation.

Stephanie's solution was simple: a weekly meeting with her boss where she took full responsibility to create the conditions in which she would operate at her best. She structured the meeting, outlined her role, listed her quarterly, monthly and weekly goals and tasks and looked to her boss for input and sign-off. Her need for structure and framework was met; her self-confidence soared; her productivity went up and she became able to function knowing she was highly rated, even though her boss never specifically gave her that feedback.

Eliciting the model is extremely straightforward. It is

simply a case of asking ourselves: *'What am I like when I am at my best? What does it look, sound and feel like to me and to others?'* We build up the model from that. It can easily be done on our own, but a friend, colleague or coach helps us notice our patterns and pushes us to get really specific in our answers. The model does not have to be technically complex. It takes different forms depending on what works for you. For some, it is a diagram or a grid. I have also seen it as a continuum or list. For others, it is enough to have talked it through. This elicits a conceptual model in their mind.

Take Jonathan. He had been in a complete stew for two days because he felt he needed more time than the hour his new boss had allotted him to explain his business plan. Jonathan's model highlighted his need for supportive environments, with enough time to build rapport and make a personal connection. Given that this was the first time he was to meet this new CEO, he felt he would be unable to perform well within the time constraints.

Once Jonathan had articulated his model, he realized that it was essential to ask the new CEO for more time. Without that, he would not do himself justice in the meeting and would fret for another two days until the meeting took place. Jonathan laughed at the ridiculousness of his anger and frustration when there was such a simple solution to hand. He phoned up, there and then, during our session. The CEO was delighted to give him more time – in fact he had believed Jonathan had set the original time parameters himself.

It was enough for Jonathan just to discuss it. He had formulated the model in his mind. He always insists now on ensuring his desired parameters are in place when he wants to ensure a high-performance meeting.

These examples show the importance of doing the groundwork in really understanding ourselves at our best. This brings knowledge from the 'unconscious incompetence' stage to the 'conscious incompetence' stage (*see* Chapter 1). This allows us to make conscious choices about change. We can see from these examples the positive impact that even the most minor amendments can make.

Choice points

Once we arrive at our model, it becomes clear that there are certain people and certain situations that bring out the best and the worst in us. Choice points are those times in the day or week when we can make a more conscious, and therefore more positive, choice about the behaviour we exhibit. Identifying choice points is often easiest when we list down the people and situations who bring out the 'not me' and then those that elicit the 'best me'. The lists quickly show up the usual suspects and we can then choose to address either the most frequent choice points or those that are less frequent but make a significant impact on our effectiveness.

I recently worked with a very interesting chap, Robert. Through some psychometric testing, we established what his interpersonal needs were. Sometimes he wanted to be around people and sometimes he absolutely did not, and needed time on his own. In itself, that's not unusual, but the extremity of his reactions was. He had lost sight of himself and was confused. He was alarmed, claiming to have a Dr Jekyll and Mr Hyde personality. His job demanded he be very sociable, and sometimes that was fine – he is a loud, larger-than-life character who can make everyone laugh just by his presence. On many occasions, he would be gregarious, walking the floor, joking and bantering with everyone he saw. On other days, however, he felt that if people came near him he'd go mad. He would snap and be moody. This was causing him a lot of problems because people were seeing him as highly inconsistent.

When we elicited his Personal Best Model, he felt legitimized. Once he understood his interpersonal requirements – the need for regular intervals of physical and personal space and the need to put boundaries round that space, both in his private life and at work – it changed how he felt about himself and how he was at work. His choice points were those times when he needed privacy yet people wanted his attention or his involvement. Now when he felt he needed to be on his own, he was calmly clear to those around him. *'Now is not a good time, could you reschedule please.'* He would take the time to work on a document, to work at home, and just by being aware of when the need for privacy came, he was able to be much truer to himself and communicate that need clearly to others. As a result, Robert came across as much more consistent because people weren't trying to cut across or violate his genuine needs. He felt better about himself because he was being more himself. And at the choice points where he felt inclusive, he chose now to be proactively and visibly sociable, walking the floor with a vengeance and firing up the troops. He milked those times for all they were worth.

Small actions

Most executives probably operate at somewhere between 60 and 85 per cent of being themselves. The balance is reclaimed by small actions. The small actions strategy is deceptively simple. It is about taking a small action at the choice point that is true to us, so enabling us to be more effective. It is not about a complete overhaul in our behaviour. It's the little tap of the chisel that gets us closer to our real selves inside.

Most people don't like radical change, we prefer it in the form of evolution. Only 20 per cent of the population are comfortable with radical change at work. The brain doesn't accommodate new ideas easily; it synthesizes new ideas with what's been known before, and categorizes them, so new concepts can be very uncomfortable. This means that big choices or big decisions are often very difficult to make and can take a long time.

But if we can put the building blocks in place and take small steps, we will reach our goal faster. I refer to the need to take mini-steps regularly. I talked in Chapter 2 about the need to break down our dreams into small actionable steps, because people, when discussing change, all too often use the analogy of jumping off a cliff. That's what it feels like to them. Like going into freefall. I, for one, would never advocate that. If we want to get to the bottom of a cliff, because that's where our goal is, the best thing isn't to take one terrifying leap, but to work our way down with a rope ladder, step by step, with a safety harness fully on. It may seem like it will take longer, but with each step we get nearer to our goal. Meanwhile, the person at the top of the cliff is still dithering, because for most people taking that one big leap is just too frightening.

Small actions have been proven to be successful strategies. Business practices have shown how effective SMART (Specific, Measurable, Achievable, Realistic, Timebound) objectives are. They work because they operate on the concept of 'chunking down', getting information, goals and ideas into bite-size, achievable chunks. Psychologists have shown that wellbeing, happiness and physical health are correlated to feeling that we can achieve things ourselves. If we feel that events outside us determine our fortune – i.e. we have an external locus of control (see Chapter 1) – we are more apt to be anxious, unwell and depressed.

By their very nature, big decisions and choices are often perceived to have external elements attached to them but the aim is to keep the locus of control internal. The 'small actions' strategy supports this. It creates easy decisions to make at the choice point and keeps the locus of control internal. The positive outcome of small actions creates success, and success, however small, breeds success. Every time we take a small action we move towards being more true to ourselves. If we let others choose for us, we are not necessarily making the best choice for ourselves.

SUMMARY

The Personal Best Model is a continuous circular process that works best when monitored and adjusted regularly. With greater awareness of us at our best, we take small steps to being at our best more often, and before long we will forget why we ever thought we should be anyone else other than ourselves.

The workplace has seen a considerable shift in that it now looks for authenticity in its leaders, and considerable emphasis is placed on attracting and celebrating diversity. There has never been a better time to be ourselves. This shift, coupled with the growing recognition of human capital, emotional intelligence and the so-called 'war for talent', is allowing people to be more true to themselves and to encourage and appreciate the unique talents of individuals.

In applying this to our own situation, we need to be brave and say: *'I don't need to be like the person who is my role model. I can be me, my version of it.'* We must recognize and honour the uniqueness in ourselves. Nobody has our personality, our relationship with our parents, our schooling, our experiences, our friends, our way of filtering the world: no one thinks like we do and therefore there is nobody that can see events, and think about them in exactly the way we do. Our unique offering gives a different perspective to anybody else's. So we must use it, we must take permission to be more true to ourselves and see this as a positive opportunity, for it is a wonderful gift. We must validate it and honour it.

In summary, the five stages of the Personal Best Model are:

Acknowledgement, the first phase, requires us to take an honest look at what we are feeling and experiencing at work and to assess how true to ourselves we are being. The corollary to this, is to acknowledge how accurate our self-awareness is. How much do we know about ourselves? It is not easy to know if we are being true to ourselves if we are not fully aware who the real we is. We may think we know ourselves well but in coaching we find that most managers and directors do not know themselves well unless they have been through some (or all) of the following:

— extensive profiling work, e.g. the looking at personality and thinking patterns through psychometric tests
— 360-degree feedback, e.g. feedback from those who work with you, report to you or manage you, i.e. feedback from all around you
— coaching, e.g. helping you to understand yourself better and work out a more effective way of working/behaving in your life
— therapy, e.g. help in dealing with issues and understanding why you are who you are and react in the way that you do.

Self-discovery, the second phase, is the self-awareness stage. Those who prefer to solve problems by internal reflection will learn most by internal dialogue, while those who learn best by talking through ideas will crystalize their thoughts through dialogue with others. The goal of this stage is to develop a full understanding of who we are *when we are at our best,* but it is useful to remember that self-awareness is a life-long journey. At this stage, we fill in any gaps in our self-awareness highlighted by the first phase. This phase leads you directly into phase three.

Copycat Here, the aim is to formulate a model using all we have learnt about ourselves at our best. Called 'modelling' by psychologists, this brings to conscious awareness all that we do subconsciously throughout our work life, enabling us to see it, hear it, feel it and talk about it. By placing language around nebulous thoughts, we make them real. What we will have is a blueprint or model of ourselves at our best. The goal now is to copy it, to behave in such a way that emulates the model we have outlined.

Choice points By formulating a model, we become aware at what points it is easier or harder to be true to ourselves. We will have highlighted the people and situations that draw forth the real we effortlessly, and we will have noticed patterns about when it is harder to be our real selves. These are called choice points and identifying these is the fourth phase of the process.

Small actions With all this information brought out of the unconscious, all that's left is to make it happen. The premise of this final phase is that this process is not about a complete overhaul of our personality but a way of being our best selves more often. By doing this we aim to bring the sense of control inside, rather than leaving it outside, which is what happens if we expect things to happen in spite of ourselves rather than because of us. This is referred to as the 'locus of control' and it has been clinically proven that those with an internal locus of control have better psychological health and wellbeing than those who have an external one.

We are then back at the beginning again, acknowledging our situation. This is a continuous process and one when exercised regularly leaves you with a renewed sense of personal power and balance.

Interactive session

Self-awareness

- What are you best at, what is your unique contribution? What is your 'gift'?
- Work with a coach or a human resources specialist to develop your self-awareness (asking for psychometric tests or profiling tools can help your understanding).
- Ask for 360-degree feedback, either formally or informally, at work and with friends.

Choice points

- List what or who triggers you to be at your best.
- List what or who triggers you to be at your worst.
- List what or who triggers the 'not you'.
- Note three choices you could make which would create more moments when you are at your best and reduce the number when you're at your worst or are 'not you.'

Rituals

- Keep a 'gratitude journal' noting things that went well during the day when you felt good about yourself.
- Keep your focus positive and keep it short so that it is a joy, not a chore.
- Notice when you were at your best.
- Notice choices that you would like to make going forward to be at your best more often.
- Do it just before you go to sleep: it sends you to sleep feeling positive.

HOW . . .
to get more balance in our lives

— by using our intuition

7

Intuition –
the Ultimate Balancer

Intuition is probably the ultimate tool in helping us achieve more balance in our lives but most of us don't use it because we either don't know how to, or we don't trust it scientifically. This chapter addresses both issues.

Intuition and work–life decisions

On returning to work full time after maternity leave, Mary, a managing director, was determined to sort out her work–life balance. Prior to the birth of her first child she had worked long hours but had now decided to arrive at the office at 8 am and leave no later than 6 pm. That way she would have one hour to bath and play with her baby before bedtime. Mary felt she had found the right work–life balance for her.

Six weeks into this new routine, the CEO called an emergency meeting at 5.30 pm. Mary spent all afternoon worrying: should she say she couldn't make it, should she go for half an hour, should she stay as long as it took? Her intuition told her to be true to her principles, but she ignored her intuition and went. She knew straightaway that she had made the wrong call. Mary watched the clock ticking, thinking *'I'll go at five past . . . ten past . . . quarter past'*. Each time the clock passed her deadline, she felt sick and she eventually left the meeting early to scornful glances from her male counterparts.

She cried all the way home and vowed that from then on she would only stay at work past six if it was her choice, or if something happened that she considered a genuine emergency. She believed she would know this by listening to and honouring her intuition. Mary swears that this is the secret of what keeps her in balance. She works full time but leaves at 6 pm every evening, unless she's cleared it with her own conscience by tuning into her intuition.

Mary's dilemma is a classic case of the pull between work and home life. Often, working mums or dads cite incidents of missing important meetings to go to a child's sports day or nativity play, but my findings suggest that it's not those big events that cause the tension between a work choice or a home life choice. Those are actually the easy decisions to make. It's the small but nonetheless important events that throw us out of balance, cause us the confusion and the guilt. Missing the baby's bath time in itself is hardly a big deal, one could argue, but it was a huge deal to Mary, because *that* bath time and *that* meeting represented a microcosm of the work–life balance issue for her. For someone else it would, of course, be something entirely different. Listening to our intuition can help ease the many, many decisions that heighten or release that tension, depending on what we decide.

Using intuition more in the workplace and our home life creates better balance. Life is about choices and decisions and, in my view, intuition plays a pivotal role in making decisions that lead to a healthy work–life balance. When tough work–life decisions loom, we can choose to listen and act on our intuition, or we can choose to ignore it and learn from it in a way that sears the point into our brain for ever – as happened with Mary. Either way, intuition will guide us to making the decision that will create a better balance between work and life when the two seem to be pulling in opposite directions.

Every executive I interviewed recounted an emotionally-charged, complex work–life dilemma, a conflict between that *crucial* work meeting and the *need* to be at home supporting someone important, be it partner, pet, parent, child or friend. The dilemmas ranged from wanting to take time off to go to school with a child who was being bullied, wanting to be at home with a pedigree cat having kittens, or wanting to be at a dying parent's bedside. In such situations, when the work–life dilemma is encapsulated in one heated, crossroads decision, intuition comes into its own as a balancer, and listening to our intuition is the only right solution.

Tough choices

Claire had just joined a company on its executive board and was keen to impress. She was told that the board was going on a bonding weekend to discuss the forthcoming annual strategy. Perfect, she thought, until she found out the date. It was her birthday weekend when her husband was taking her for a much-needed romantic weekend. It was the first time they had had together in three years since their first child was born. It was already booked and paid for. What should she do?

Judy was a member of the executive board and had been with the company about six months. Every summer the chairman threw a party at his house but the event coincided with her annual holiday, the flights were booked, her husband had booked time off work. What should she do?

Well . . . Claire said no to the executive bonding and strategizing and went on her romantic weekend, and Judy changed the dates of her holiday to be at the party. Neither of these senior women is with those companies any longer, both moving on through choice. Both are still happily married. Which of them was right and which was wrong?

They were both right . . . for them. There is no right or wrong. All that matters is that they made the right decision for them. Claire would have felt wrong letting her husband down, while going on holiday and missing that party would have made Judy feel bad and more out of balance than changing her holiday. At the time, I thought Judy was as mad as a March hare to move a holiday for her boss's party, and told her so, but that was before I realized the importance of making your own decision and of being in control of it. Changing your holiday dates doesn't throw you out of balance . . . if it's your choice to do so.

These situations demonstrate the type of constant decision-making pressure we are under. Some of the choices we have to make are small, such as what meetings we attend or what we prioritize. Others are emotionally-charged decisions where we are seemingly forced to make a clear-cut choice between home life and the workplace. But by seeing these situations in such black-and-white terms, we tend to over-dramatize the situation. If we are true to ourselves and make decisions by listening to our intuition, we can get the balance right; ignore intuition and things get out of balance big time.

Intuition in business

Intuition is becoming more widely accepted in the business world as a key ingredient in senior players' decision-making processes. CEOs may call it a hunch, inspiration or gut instinct, but more and more it is accepted that any problem-solving model has to allow for intuition. In my opinion, it is the best problem-solver we may ever find. It helps us make decisions effortlessly. It keeps us on track. It keeps us sane. It preserves our integrity. Listening to it slows us down, and, conversely, through that very process speeds us up.

Some believe that intuitive people are blessed with some kind of psychic gift. My view? We are *all* intuitive but some have mastered listening to their intuition more than others. It is a continuum with mastery at one end and disbelief at the other. I think we move from disbelief, through healthy scepticism, to tentative trust, to confident trust and then to mastery.

Disbelief	Healthy Scepticism	Tentative Trust	Confident Trust	Mastery

Intuition continuum

In my experience, most people reside somewhere between the healthy scepticism and the tentative trust, and have a desire to move towards mastery. I see my role as being to help move them along the continuum. I have met very few people, just one or two, who sit at the disbelief end, and I have been lucky enough to meet a few with impressive mastery.

Moving along the intuition continuum

So what is intuition? How do we know we can use it and trust it? How do we move along the continuum? We all use intuition and we all want more of it, we just don't necessarily know what to call it or how to explain it.

Intuition is defined in the dictionary as instinctive knowledge or insight without conscious reasoning. Others call it instinct or gut feeling, and although I believe intuition is the name we should give it, I also believe that what is most important is not what we call it, but how we explain it. If we can't explain it, we can't trust it. If we can't trust it, we can't use it, and if we can't use it, we are missing a vital tool in the kitbag for creating more balance in our lives.

If we trust our intuition, balance will follow. Why? Because it makes us look inside ourselves for the answer, because it takes our locus of control internally and because it validates our rightness. Our intuition helps us stay on course, ensuring that we don't get buffeted about too much when we are trying to find more balance in life. And perhaps most importantly it slows us down. In order to listen to our intuition, our gut feelings, our instincts, we need to slow down.

I arrived home one day to find, as I got out of the car, great scratches all down its side, scratches which hadn't been there when I got in. I hadn't parked anywhere, just dropped off a friend, so I know nobody had scraped me. As I re-lived the journey in my mind, I remembered talking animatedly to my friend, applying make-up, answering a mobile phone, all while having the music on fairly loud. I remembered having a few close encounters, as you do squeezing through London's busy streets, and I realized with a sinking heart what had happened. I'd clearly been merrily scraping my way through the streets, not hearing a sound or feeling a knock and undoubtedly leaving furious drivers in my wake not to mention wrecking my car. I learned a lot from that journey.

If we want to really notice what's going on, we need to slow down, quieten down, calm down, to only do one thing at a time. Listening to our intuition is like that. We don't have to meditate, we don't even have to take long about it, but we need to quieten down metaphorically or physically to hear what our intuition has to say.

We should regularly check in with ourselves and ask *'how do I feel about that?'* What bodily sensations am I noticing about that decision, that conversation? What sense do I have of that person? And we need to notice our responses. We must slow down to ask and slow down to listen, otherwise we will find ourselves careering through life, picking up scrapes and scratches along the way that we hardly even notice until after the event, harming and infuriating ourselves and others as we recklessly speed on.

We want to know we can trust our intuition. When we know we can believe our instincts, our gut feeling, it liberates us. We don't have to search any more for the right decision, just the right-for-me-now decision.

Making sense of intuition –
some explanations

Many of my clients want to be able to believe in intuition, but feel it is too nebulous, too 'new age' or just a little irresponsible to tune into a supposed 'higher self' to pick up a message that may or may not be correct. I share with them some explanations from the cognitive psychologists' interpretation of intuition. These explanations worked for me. They stripped me of my own disbelief and liberated me to find a new level of trust in myself. In doing so, I was able to let go of the rational, cognitive explanations and be more open to intuition in its widest sense. Now I am confident about my intuition and I notice all the ways in which it helps and guides me. I believe intuition gives us the answers to the questions we're asking, it is the voice that says *'yes, that's right'* and claps silently to support and nurture our decisions. I believe intuition is about trust; trusting that we are wise and that our wisdom is worth listening to.

Intuition – calming the inner dialogue

When I lose things now, I no longer frenetically search every place three times, going around the house like a headless chicken. I stop and tune in to my intuition. In those few moments I get a sense, firstly, of whether I have truly lost the object, or whether it is just temporarily mislaid. Invariably, I get the response that it is the latter and then I calm down. I've moved from hearing that accusatory inner dialogue that goes something like: *'You idiot, you've lost it, now you're going to have to go and buy another one, you're going* to be really late now, why are you so useless?' to a calmer, more soothing voice, *'I wouldn't have done anything stupid. It's not lost, it's here. I must have put it somewhere that made sense at that time.'* Moments later I find it. It never fails. Calm, trusting and supportive, intuition is the ultimate balancer.

To me, intuition is the link between the enormity of what we are as humans, which none of us really comprehends, and the day-to-day act of normal life. Listening to intuition reminds us in one fell swoop of how much more we know than we think we know. It signals to us the infinite possibilities that the human mind can create. We can be more than we think we are if we trust our inner tutor.

Intuition – referencing life's experiences

The explanation that grounds intuition for many of my clients as a genuinely reliable business or decision-making tool is that of the cognitive psychologists. In America, a professor, Dr Gary Klein, has been following people in high-risk careers, in which do-or-die decisions have to be made, in order to see how they make decisions that often fly in the face of rules or standard procedures. He has worked with fire-fighters and nurses in intensive care units looking at how they make the critical decisions in the heat of the moment.

He found that people attributed their life-saving decisions to intuition or gut feeling. Klein concluded that 'intuition' really relates to the experience these people have. In their minds, they are filtering out the information from previous experiences, accessing data, information and memories they haven't even consciously processed. It's as if our brain swiftly runs through a Rolodex of experiences related to this one and sends a signal that we should act in a certain way. The relatively recent finding of 'thinking' cells in the gut/stomach has proved that the bodily sensations that often accompany strong intuitive feelings may be more relevant then we first thought.

This professor's work has been highlighted in business magazines and it sums up beautifully the cognitive psychologists' school of thought. Where Klein has been smart is by taking the experiments out of the lab and into the real world. That's when it gets interesting. Other business literature increasingly acknowledges the role of the gut, or intuition, in decision-making. Listening to intuition was cited recently in an article in the *Harvard Business Review* as the 'x-factor', that intangible, something special that separates the men from the boys in making superlative career enhancing decisions as they climb the corporate ladder.

The theory follows that in a business situation one should expose people to as many experiences as possible, as quickly as possible, so that they have a wider mental Rolodex. The brain records every experience and even though we can't 'remember' them, they are there. What Klein found in his work was that junior fire-fighters, pilots and nurses feel they have to mentally go through the rule book, and are therefore 'slower' and less accurate in their decision-making than people who've had more experiences, who seem to be able to instinctively go to the right one. So trust your body and your mind. Trust that what we access and are conscious of on a day-to-day basis is only a tiny fraction of what is really going on inside our heads.

Experiences allow us to make inferences and those inferences are what some call intuition. Whatever we call it, it works. We are constantly processing information unconsciously, and so we often have a sense of knowing something already that we are being told on a conscious level for the first time. We often find ourselves resonating with something, because we already know it. So when we access intuition we are accessing a lifetime of unconsciously processed information, and wow, is there a lot of information there!

Cognitive psychologists have conducted many studies on intuition and decision-making and they often conclude that visual and verbal cues are so rapidly and subliminally observed that their contribution to the final decision is virtually forgotten. Other psychologists take this a step further by saying what we are accessing is not just our lifetime of experiences, but all of humanity's experiences. This comes from Jung's theory of the 'collective unconscious'. His term is based on the notion that while every human is unique, our unconscious mind taps into the generalities of humanity in the collective unconscious, which is why, at points in history, certain ideas, symbols or theories take hold at the same time, regardless of race, belief or geographical location.

Jung's theory of the 'collective unconscious' was coolly received in the 1920s but is now considered an enormous contribution to psychology and is growing in popularity. Thus, when we listen to our intuition – i.e. go beyond conscious reasoning – we access the universal knowledge and insight of all mankind. If this seems unlikely to you, then stay with the first explanation. All that matters is that you make sense of what intuition is in real, everyday, tangible terms. When you've made sense of it you'll use it more, and your scepticism will be replaced with tentative trust, and before you know it, you'll be moving along that continuum beautifully!

How many senses do we have?

I read a crime novel once where the detective (I believe it was Hercule Poirot!) was able to astound a new client by appearing to be psychic, telling him what he'd eaten for breakfast that morning and what his financial situation was and that he had been in a hurry when he left the house. After the client has left, the detective explains to his slow-witted sidekick that he'd in fact identified it all by using extreme powers of observation: there was a trace of egg on the man's tie, there was something about the way his coat was buttoned up, his socks didn't match, his suit was of good quality but very old-fashioned.

Intuition is our sixth sense and is accessed via our other senses that are in turn under-utilized. Eyes are brain tissue and, just by following where somebody's eyes move, you can tell what they are thinking about. If a person's eyes are directed up, it means they're visualizing something; eyes down, they are accessing a feeling or a personal emotion; eyes to the side means they are listening to something internally. We need to open our eyes, open our ears, open all our senses, because in doing so we access our sixth sense, intuition.

As intuition and instinct become more accepted in society, this 'sixth sense' will soon be considered commonplace. If we access our sixth sense in the same way the detective did, purely by increasing the use of our five other senses, then we are improving our ability to assimilate information and understand more with very little effort.

Intuition is information is power

As we improve our observation and sensing skills we immediately gain more information. In business, this means power. In meetings, accentuating our observation skills enables us to 'tune in' to what others are 'thinking'. It doesn't matter if we pick this up through non-verbal cues, tonality or through psychic transference of thoughts, what matters is that we are not glossing over the information we have available to our conscious minds. We are bringing to the conscious level all the things we know instinctively, intuitively.

It's great to start to test our theories. When we meet a client for the first time we can make a note of all the things we gauge about them from the first meeting. Notice what they're wearing and how they're wearing it, what type of pen they are using, whether they have a small bag or a large one, seem organized or like to go with the flow, what they say or don't say. We astound ourselves at how long the list is, what we pick up, hardly consciously registering it, and what we can infer from this surprising list of 'facts'. If we refer back to it when we know more about the client, we will be amazed by our accuracy.

When we start trusting our consistency we can start to intrigue people with how much we 'know' about them on just a quick meeting. Like the detective, they will assume we are psychic or intuitive or just incredibly clever. In studies people showed an uncannily high sense of picking up on whether people were in relationships or happy or healthy. My personal favourite is that I am always tuned into how happy someone is in their role at work. I can intuit this within five minutes of meeting someone. It's all there, laid out for us to see. Wake up, open up, our sixth sense is just waiting to be actualized.

Permission to be intuitive

Everyone has a story about some strong intuitive behaviour they have experienced first hand or that they have been on the receiving end of. It may have been a premonition, a dream, a sense of knowing what will happen next or who'll be on the phone; it may even have been as a result of a visit to a psychic, healer or medium. We want intuition to exist, and it does, but all that really matters is how we access it, how we use it more. What, to my mind, doesn't matter is how we explain it, as long as that explanation gives permission to use intuition and trust it. If the cognitive psychologists' explanation (that our lives' experiences are Rolodexed and accessed) makes sense to us, then great, we should use it. If it is the explanation of the detective and the heightened powers of observation that actually allow us to 'know' more than is seemingly normal, that's great, and if it is our belief that we are receiving messages from a Jungian collective unconscious, the universe, angels or spirit guides, then that's great too.

What matters is to pay attention to our intuition, to note down when it helps us, to tell stories about it to friends and family. We can start to say to ourselves and others: '*I'm very intuitive. Once I . . .*' and tell the story, because we will have a story. We *are* intuitive, we all are, and not using our intuition causes us to live a life without a vital amount of information. The information that helps us make the right choices about how to do what's right for us. When we do what's right, we feel calm, when we do what's right, we feel good. Feeling good and calm are pre-requisites for balance.

Doing what's right creates balance

Last year a CEO asked me to coach someone in his very large organization. I had my diagnostic session with him, a prickly, at first easy-to-dislike man. I sensed there was something very wrong – human nature is not naturally antagonistic. He reminded me of a hedgehog that rolls itself up into a ball at the slightest hint of danger. During our session he unrolled, smoothing his prickles and exposing the vulnerable, loving, caring man underneath, who desperately wanted to be respected, liked and included. His opening gambit was that he was expecting to be promoted to number two in the company and wanted me to help him deal with this situation. By the end of our session, however, he had revealed that he was in fact terrified of being fired and he knew really that he wasn't in the running for that position at all. We agreed that the coaching programme should work on his relationship with his CEO – he found it hard to be himself around him – and on making him more confident and clear about his role in the company.

Soon after that first session, I had a call from his boss to say they were going to let him go and could I postpone my next session with him. I agreed, but as I put down the phone I felt physically sick. I had bonded with Mark, I couldn't phone up with some flimsy excuse. I felt in such a dilemma, but I had to listen to my body, my gut. I phoned back his boss and said I wasn't prepared to lie. If they wanted the session postponed they must do it at their end. They didn't like it, but they agreed, and one year on Mark is not only still with the company but he's been promoted, has regained his confidence and enjoyed a much better relationship with his CEO, up to the time that the CEO himself was ousted.

Is that intuition or is it just a matter of integrity? I'm not sure it matters, but what interested me was my extreme bodily response? Why the instinct that I mustn't do it? I had to do something about it, even if it jeopardized my role with that CEO and the company. Agreeing to that work and 'lying' to my client would have knocked me out of balance. It would have taken up more headspace than you can imagine. I'd have lost sleep, felt guilty, taken it out on others, resented the CEO, been angry at myself. What hope do we have for inner calm with that onslaught of negative energy? Forget it. We must listen to our gut, our heart, our intuition and do the right thing in line with the messages we hear. Then, and only then, will we feel in that calm place of balance.

Intuition as an aid for internal politics

One of my clients, Alison, was working hard on launching an independent company, spinning a division out of its parent company. After months of internal presentations, cost benefit analyses and launch plans delivered to apparent full support, the project seemed to have ground to a halt. Alison was tearing her hair out. Motivation and morale was sinking fast and she felt if they didn't launch the company in the next quarter they would miss their competitive advantage. When I arrived for our session, she was angry, exasperated and had lost all her energy. She was at a loss how to make it happen.

I discouraged her from producing yet another Power Point presentation about the need to launch urgently. Instead, we used her intuition to ascertain where the real blocks were coming from with the major stakeholders. We went through each of them, ranking them as supporter or detractor based on what they claimed to be. Then we did a similar list based on her intuition and compared the two. There was one person who was outwardly claiming to be a supporter, but Alison's intuition told her otherwise. She sensed he was a detractor and had somehow become the block to the launch. Alison listened to her intuition and the next day confronted this person, who after blustering through the first part of the meeting admitted his reservations and agreed he had not been putting his weight behind it internally. Alison was able to get him on her side again and the company was launched with his support. It happened three months later than Alison wanted, but still ahead of all their competitors.

Intuition as a lifesaver

I have devoted a whole chapter to intuition because I believe it plays a vital role in creating a balanced life. Balance comes from inside, as does intuition. The biggest concern most people have with intuition – once they accept they want to access it – is how to be sure it's actually intuition speaking and not some other internal rogue voice. As a rule of thumb, if it energizes us it's intuition, if it deadens us it's not.

Accessing intuition is merely a case of slowing down, listening, looking, opening up our senses and being willing to trust that we know much more than we are aware of knowing. The signs are all there, the gut feeling, the feeling sick when things are wrong, the energy when we are doing the right thing, the excitement when we're on track, or the sinking feeling when we know we've made the wrong choice. It's just a case of allowing the information in. In doing so we save our lives, not in the dramatic sense of life versus death, but in the sense of saving our lives as they are meant to be, dynamically balanced and full of meaning.

I have a very strong metaphorical vision of intuition as a dolphin, and while I was writing this chapter I shared this thought with my researcher, Kelly. I told her because I know she loves dolphins. Kelly in turn told me a story about her sister that so astonished me that I wanted to share it, because to me it sums up the role I see intuition playing in our lives. It is a true story and was reported in all the newspapers in New Zealand when it happened a few years ago.

Kelly's sister, Anna, had always wanted to swim the Cook Strait, the 26-kilometre stretch of ocean between the North and South Islands of New Zealand. Anna trained mentally and physically for months for the challenge and on a calm but cold day she set off at 5.30 am from South Island. Although cold, the conditions were good, with low wind and the swell relatively flat. Anna was prepared for a maximum swim time of eight hours, which she was confident she could do. A contributing factor for attempting the feat was Anna's dream of swimming with dolphins in their natural habitat on equal terms.

Her first encounter with dolphins was four and a half hours into the swim. She could hear their sonar clicks before she could see them. There were about ten of them in the pod and they swam with her for about an hour. The dolphins' social behaviour was evident in their constant playfulness. They would pair up and dive down really deep and then come straight up and jump out in front of her. They always swam just out of touching distance and Anna felt an immense joy as her dream was slowly unfolding. She communicated with them by talking and making noises underwater and they would answer her back.

Her second encounter was entirely different. Anna had now been swimming for ten and a half hours, past her estimated maximum time as unexpected tidal changes had pulled her way off course. She was fatigued and hypothermic, dehydrated and nearing exhaustion, but battling on, dedicated to achieving her goal. Two support boats accompanied Anna on her swim, a small inflatable with a navigator and swim coach, and a larger launch with extra navigators and a captain. The small boat was constantly in Anna's view as she breathed to the left. When, at a certain point, she saw them looking intently at the water, she sensed something was wrong. She breathed to the right to see the other launch powering off in another direction. Her coach banged the bottom of the boat, the signal for Anna to stop swimming immediately. She wanted to know why, desperate to finish her swim.

There was a shark heading straight for Anna and the launch was trying to lead it away by getting it to take a line. The situation was tense. If the danger couldn't be eliminated in the next few minutes the swim would be cancelled. Then from the distance, came a huge pod of dolphins. None of the experienced navigators and seamen on board who had travelled the Strait for more than 30 years had ever seen so many dolphins together in a pod. There were over 300 of them, coming towards Anna like a herd of galloping horses in a desert. Anna again heard them before she saw them. As they came, they surrounded her, behind, in front, and below, placing themselves between her and the shark. And this time, there was no playful behaviour, the dolphins just swam slowly and steadily with Anna and she felt an amazing bond and sense of safety and protection. The inspiration kept her focused to swim and the dolphins drove the shark away.

The swim pushed Anna beyond her limits, but she was exhilarated, she had gone beyond her believed capabilities, and she'd fulfilled her dream. She'd crossed the Strait and connected with the dolphins in the most magical and extraordinary way.

To me, that sums up exactly how I think intuition works with us. It uplifts us, inspires us and encourages us, yet saves us from danger, protecting us and becoming serious when necessary. It supports us and nurtures our journey, balancing us through choppy waters, ensuring that through the rough and tumble of the waves we are washed up laughing and exhilarated on the shore, safe and unresisting. That's how I visualize intuition: a smiling, beautiful, friendly helper, gracefully helping us to safety, building gratitude and trust in us that bonds us for ever. Why wouldn't we use it?

SUMMARY

Trust your intuition, gut feeling, instinct, whatever you want to call it. It's a frequently heard message, but one that is fundamental to the journey towards work–life balance. For it comes from deep inside us, requiring us to slow down and look inside ourselves, and it is impossible to access if we are caught on the frenetic treadmill of a life that's out of balance. It can help in all aspects of life, too, from major corporate decisions to everyday home ones. Don't ignore it, for unless we tune into our internal messaging service we can't hope to reach our ultimate goal of balance.

Interactive session

The intuition continuum
- Think about where you sit on the intuition continuum and where you would like to be.
- What else do you need to know or do to move yourself up the continuum?

Solve a problem using intuition
- Think about a problem/challenge you are currently facing at work. Close your eyes, take some time to tune into your intuition about the solution. You do not necessarily have to heed it at this point. Make a note in a safe place of what your intuition told you, then leave it. Look back at it once you've made your decision, and look at what hindsight can tell you about your intuition and the decision you ultimately made. As time goes on and more events unfold, its always interesting to revisit this.

Rituals

- Think each evening as you finish work how your intuition helped you during the working day.
- Make notes of first impressions of people and refer back to them when you know them better.

HOW . . .
to get more balance in our lives

— by choosing health

8

The Choice to be Well

Balance lies within us. It's in our minds and our minds, of course, are linked to our bodies. It follows, then, that a balanced mind is a balanced body, and that an out-of-balance body is an out-of-balance mind.

My message in this chapter is simple: that we have choices about our health because there is irrefutable proof (and stories abound) of apparently miracle cures and the ability of the mind to heal the body. I'm told the mind–body interface is now one of the hottest new areas of medical science. Considerable research has been done into the links between our immune systems and our endocrine and nervous systems, leaving previously sceptical scientists to conclude that there is no separation between mind and body.

The concept of friends and family having illnesses that are psychosomatic is one that is common and acceptable to us all. Some doctors, particularly those in alternative fields, believe that most, if not all, illnesses are psychosomatic. In her revolutionary book, *Molecules of Emotion*, Dr Candace Pert tells the wonderful story of her discovery of chemical substances in our bodies, which prove the links. Her story also details her conversion from hard core scientist to being a frontline mind–body expert. Detailed so scientifically, it is compelling evidence of the power the mind has over the body. As Pert points out, 'psyche' comes from the Greek meaning breath/soul, and 'soma' from the Greek for 'body', so a disease that is considered psychosomatic is one that affects mind, body and soul.

I firmly believe that good health includes the question of mind over matter or, as body–mind experts position it, mind is matter. They are one and the same. Getting ill represents an out-of-balance mind and body, while getting better can balance the mind as the body regains its equilibrium. It doesn't matter whether the problem first manifests itself physically or psychologically, because the two are inextricably linked. A malfunctioning body is a body not aligned to its energy sources, its fuel and its balance. The malfunction is a message to the brain to slow down, take notice, to choose balanced health. Clearly environmental and genetic factors play a role in sickness, but so does the mind, which is the part we often forget to treat when we ask for medical help.

Employees in virtually every company I work with regale me with stories of sickness, days in bed, exhaustion and stress. The workforce is blighted by stress, costing the economy millions. The healthy, energetic balanced self is being replaced by a tired and lethargic or frenzied substandard one, one that's shrunk in size. I see our bodies as vessels, as buckets of wellness. All too often this bucket is filled with mud and dirt, but when we rummage around in the sludge we can find grains of mercurial brightness that can startle with their shining silver, their fluid freedom. Our bucket of wellness, our natural energy, should be just that: a silver mercurial liquid that is strong yet fluid.

If we can plunge the murky depths and bear the mucky

touch, we should sift through the sludge of ill health to separate it from the mercury. The murk and the muck are blighting and hiding our true health. What is this sludge? It's the caffeine that has solidified, the nicotine that has blackened and stained, the alcohol that's fermented into rot, the awful foods and the damaging drugs that have concocted a potion to make us feel slow, ill and heavy. Our energy is hidden deep in that bucket of wellness, deep beneath the mud. Let's dig it out and make it work for us!

Drop the caffeine, drop the booze, and sort out the food, for this sludgy way of life is not the one we're supposed to be leading. The strange little niggles we feel, the tiredness and discomfort are all hints of this, so sluice away the sludge to find the silver, the quickness and the mercurial spirit of a human being in full health and balance, a body in equipoise. Let's notice our strong limbs that carry us to work and back, up and down stairs, around the houses, to the sports field, to the gym. Remember our backs, as strong as a rod, rendering us upright as part of our unique biped birthright. Give credit to our feet that carry this strong upright frame and walk on this earth leaving our mark for all to see. Let our footsteps show the spring in the step of a mercurial spirit that's free. For our steps have become weighed down by the sludge and mud and they leave a mark that is sorry, tired, dead and slow.

The substandard health we accept as the norm is not how it should be. The aches, the pains, the sleepless nights, the irritable bowel syndrome, the virus alerts, the skin flare-ups – these are all messages alerting us that we're running on empty and need to be refuelled. We should replenish more regularly, nurture our health and take care of ourselves, because a balanced body is the key to vitality. A balanced life will never come out of a body that's running on empty.

The impact of stress on the immune system is well documented. Numerous studies have shown the importance of a positive mental attitude in the resistance of disease, and the power of touch and kind words in recovery. A study in Sweden even introduced playful 'massage' between school children. Fully-clothed, the children drew letters on each other's back, made pretend pizzas, planted gardens, visited a zoo. The results were dramatic: there was less fighting and aggression, less bullying, children asked rather than snatched and there was a notable improvement in concentration and performance. Our bodies want to be touched, nurtured, cared for. When they are, they respond by demonstrating better behaviour and more positive emotions.

Tiredness, lethargy, lack of energy and insomnia are all signs that things aren't right. Do *not* accept them as the norm. Freneticism, manic speech, extreme impatience, intolerance are all signs that we are stressed. This is not right. A happy, balanced human being is not meant to behave like that. When the body becomes ill, don't ignore it. I don't mean we should go home, have two days off work and feel that we've looked after ourselves. This is dealing with the situation on one level – but *only* on one level. We need to find out what has *caused* the imbalance, what physical and emotional issues need to be addressed. In many cases, the work–life balance that we seek could manifest itself after just a few tiny changes to the way we look after ourselves physically and a small acknowledgement of the emotions that are eating away at our sense of wellbeing. The first step is to notice how we handle ourselves physically at work.

Take Will, a busy television producer, who rarely stops for a lunchbreak, doesn't see daylight from the moment he arrives at the office at 8 am until he leaves after 7 pm, drinks coffee after coffee during the day and eats biscuit after biscuit in meetings. He's exhausted, resentful and, by his own admission, unproductive. He suffers from insomnia and recurrent bouts of tonsillitis and flu. He is too exhausted to see friends. He hates where he lives. It's always a mess but he has no time to get a cleaner or, more importantly, to achieve his dream of owning a flat with a garden. His savings are piled up in the bank, the streets he'd like to live on are highlighted, but there's no time to do anything about it, so he just sits tight and feels worse every day. He cancels friends regularly, putting pressure on relationships and causing him untold guilt. He has what he describes as an 'invisible in-tray' at home. Its contents are never addressed and this builds up more shame, frustration and guilt at all that is left undone in his personal life. His working habits are *so* poor that they produce highly ineffective behaviour, namely disorganized thinking, bad use of time, and a feeling of being overwhelmed by the simplest of tasks.

We worked on his health, his working style, and explored the impact of the guilt and stress to improve the madness in his day. Will started actioning a few small things to break the cycle of unproductive working and ill health. He dropped his caffeine intake, walks outside at least once a day, makes a trip to something uplifting twice a week in his lunchbreak (a park, gallery, shops, reading in a café), uses his commute to make phone calls (to friends or to pay bills), works for periods of 120 minutes maximum before stretching and walking round the office. And he has started to take time to address his 'invisible in-tray' and focus his attention on achieving some home wins, such as getting a cleaner and buying a flat. He rightly saw these areas as essential to achieving full health and productivity, rather than some indulgence he couldn't allow himself.

Six months on, Will is a productive, promoted and happy home-owner who works fewer hours, gets more done and feels in control – and he's had a clean bill of health to boot.

Self-care – irresponsible or responsible?

Taking care of ourselves should be easy, shouldn't it? So what's the block? The biggest one is the feeling that it is somehow *irresponsible* to focus on improving self-care. It feels selfish, indulgent, like a distraction from the real issue.

But, surely, if we are relaxed, happy, balanced, healthy, are we not more likely to be able to respond effectively to whatever the world throws at us? Of course we are. Our ability to respond improves and that's what being truly responsible is about – *being able to respond*.

Tiredness, irritability and feeling sorry for ourselves gets us nowhere with our boss, our colleagues, clients, partner, friends or children. Feeling fresh, invigorated and energized does. So do whatever it takes to get you there. Have a massage, play a round of golf, take a walk, visit an art gallery or enjoy a long bath. Just do it and feel no guilt about doing it. Why should we feel guilty about improving our ability to respond? We shouldn't. Self-indulgence, self-care, self-nurturing is our responsibility, and by taking on that responsibility we are doing everyone around us a favour. Remember joy, contentment and other positive emotions help increase our resourcefulness, so we must take responsibility for diarying events that will boost us not drain us. That way we become more effective.

If you don't believe this approach will deliver, try a little experiment. Take a week where you add self-care to the 'to-do' list. Make it happen, then sit back and watch as your relationships improve, you look and feel better, you like yourself more – and, hey!, look how much easier things seem.

Look out for the coincidences:

- the e-mail that comes in with good news while we're off doing something 'for ourselves'
- the phone calls that come in when we've rearranged our office to be a nicer environment
- the great conversations that flow because we went for lunch rather than straight to the next meeting
- the brilliant idea that came when we went to that film/art gallery/treatment.

All of these coincidences have happened to me and many have happened to my clients when I encourage them to take notice for themselves.

Self-care is important for balance because, if nothing else, it stops us becoming self-righteous martyrs. If we feel 'given-to', we are more ready to give. New habits of self-care help us be resilient. If we are running on reserves, we have little to offer, we are brittle. Let us be that beautiful, nourished green leaf that bounces back to its original shape after being squashed in our hands. Don't be the dry brown leaf that cracks and breaks under the softest of touches. Balanced living means looking after our health, which means looking after both our body *and* mind. We will never be in control of our lives and our work–life balance if we are not in control of ourselves. It starts and ends with us.

Most of this book deals with exercises for the mind, which will positively impact on our health, but this chapter includes some simple suggestions to improve our physical health. None more so than that followed by one of my clients, who I saw whilst I was writing this chapter. She is a very successful managing director of a large company, she was glowing and radiant with clarity of purpose. Something was different. She'd been de-toxing for a month, consuming no caffeine or alcohol. *'It scares me,'* she said, *'how clear-headed I feel. I normally drink half a bottle of wine each night and coffee throughout the day.'* She admitted she was in an evangelical stage and would no doubt return to both caffeine and alcohol, but never to the same level as before, for her life had become so much clearer, she'd emerged from the fog. The clarity and vision were making life too easy, too balanced to relinquish.

Now I am a big fan of those two little evils, caffeine and alcohol, and consider them a natural and fun part of life. I'm not advocating total abstinence, just an appreciation of what life can be like when we reduce our intake and see the world as it really is. Caffeine and alcohol are both big factors in raising stress levels, as medical studies constantly show. It's this simple. Drinking four or five coffees a day makes the body act as if it were under constant stress. As American professor James Lane, who has conducted some of these studies, said: *'Moderate caffeine consumption makes a person react as if he or she is having a very stressful day.'*

The logic is simple. Caffeine increases stress levels, and stress reduces the immune system and makes you susceptible to illnesses. Sustained stress leads directly to stress-related diseases such as irritable bowel syndrome, psoriasis, increased blood pressure, stomach disorders and so on. Am I scare-mongering? I don't think so. We all know the dangers of alcohol, drugs, uppers, downers, sleeping pills. Caffeine is a stealth aggressor to our wellbeing. I used to drink six, maybe eight coffees a day. I didn't mean to, but I'd have a couple in the morning before work, one at my desk and then one or two during every meeting. It all built up. I never felt its effects, and all that 'it makes me climb the walls' business that others more moderate in their intake would claim used to drive me mad. But the truth is, we do not know the effect it is having on our body. We're in denial. We're speeding along on a crazy high, without a hope of hearing or feeling reality kick in.

My own conversion came through a painful experience with my daughter. My two-year-old was in agony again with severe constipation. With four or five days between toilet visits, even with laxatives, she was in acute pain and it was breaking my heart. She was being sent home from nursery and she couldn't enjoy anything because she'd be either writhing around in pain, or walking around in a panicked and distracted way. We'd seen the GP and been referred to the best children's hospital in the country. She'd been through intensive and invasive tests under heavy sedatives, we'd been to the osteopath, the ayurvedic clinic, and the homeopath. Nothing was helping. It was only when my own coach, who has a very holistic approach, encouraged me to make the link between my daughter's health and my own that things started to shift in my mind. How could this be?

At the time, I had just started my own company and was racing around very preoccupied. I was working three days a week, an apparently balanced split between work and home life, but I was out of balance internally. I was manic and hectic and my daughter's behaviour was wild, loud and intense. A naturally sweet and gentle girl and usually a joy to be around, she was at this time hyper, high-pitched and hard to control.

I made some significant changes to my life. I sorted out my working life by taking on associates to help with the work-load, changing my diary management and halving the number of clients. But the change I am convinced made the biggest difference was that I stopped drinking caffeine eight times a day and replaced it with herbal teas and water. The effect was extraordinary and almost instantaneous. It's not difficult to see why – drinking eight cups of coffee was like having a bucketload of stress thrown at me every day. I calmed down, my daughter's behaviour became better almost overnight and she returned to being the adorable, energetic, enthusiastic girl she truly is. Her constipation improved swiftly as we rebalanced, mother and daughter, family united. The busy-ness went out of the business, and a joyous, slow richness replaced it. Bizarrely, with fewer clients and a calmer work schedule, I earned more in the next six months than I had done in the previous six. In my slowing down I had speeded up, and by nurturing my body and hers, she became totally healed.

I have not completely given up coffee, but my intake is now a maximum of one cup a day and usually rarely that. Decaffeinated coffee is my preferred choice and I note the caffeine content in other drinks and chocolate and take that into my quota too. I know for sure now that she and I are connected in our healing, but that knowledge is intuitive and instinctive rather than proven scientifically.

I am convinced that many illnesses are a manifestation of a mental or emotional disease, of a mind and body out of balance, and that often they can be healed through the mind. I am not claiming it is all in the mind, as environment and genetics certainly play their part. What is obvious to me, however, is that we underestimate the role of the mind; research clearly shows that it plays a much larger role in our health than most of us have ever been taught. The body can be healed from the inside and outside, so let us acknowledge more the inside-out approach, so we can blend its ways with our science successes. We can heal ourselves and heal our minds, for a balanced body is a balanced mind.

In his talks and books about the ageing process, Deepak Chopra, who has done much to popularize integrated medicine and highlighted the incredible healing power of the mind, claims that ageing is in fact a social construct, that 'old' is something we teach ourselves to be. We're all in it together, he argues, convincing each other and agreeing that this is what 'old' does. It gets weak and it dies. I loved the story I heard him relate about a young American psychologist, Ellen Langer, who ran a time experiment. She took 100 elderly people to a monastery and recreated a 1950s environment with 1950s magazines, furniture, television, clothes and regalia. The participants were told to act as if they were living then. Within a few days all had got 'younger' as measured by the biological markers of age such as skin elasticity, muscle tone and blood pressure. More incredible still, when they returned to their homes, they all returned to their former 'age'.

So ageing is not just a biological onslaught that we can do nothing about. Our ageing is some sort of belief that this is how we behave at a certain age. Chopra calls it the 'collective hypnosis' that we are all in. The mind has more power over the body than we had ever reckoned on.

Body messaging service

If the mind can help heal the body, it follows that we can make choices about our health. If we are ill, our body, a manifestation of what's going on inside, sends a message that all is not right. But by the time the body is screaming, the engine's grinding and the car is juddering to a halt it's too late just to fill up the tank because the damage has been done inside. We all know this intellectually – the phrase 'mind–body' is bandied around a lot – but what do we really understand of the concept? Have we always known it or do we only half know it, because somehow we can't seem to do the right things about it?

I am the worst culprit, because I know I know. I have done extensive reading and research in this area and I revel in stories of miracle cures, of cancers besieged by nutrition and holistic health and a dream of wellness that carries the victim from the deathbed to the typewriter to share their experience. Triumph over tragedy, I love it, I am a convert. But though I've read the stories and had the proof, I still ignore that dropping gauge in myself.

Let me share a story with you. First, there was the sore throat, then the laryngitis, then the hacking cough. The cough caused the sprained back, which hit at the same time as blood was found in the urine, in the same week that a tooth cracked and had to be removed, and just before the eye infection. At that point, I cracked. I know you are trying to give me a message, body, but what is it saying? The trouble with accepting the mind/body link is that nothing is ever a simple ailment any more. It is the body's text messaging service. Couldn't reach you by phone, e-mail, so wham! In comes a text message, quick, to the point and pretty unavoidable.

My problem is that I'm supposed to be writing a chapter on mind–body health links and here I am in an extreme run of ill health. I can't write on the subject while in such a sorry state. What a fraud. *'You know what?'* said my friends, hearing me whinge about it once too often. *'That's exactly why you should write it now, while you're in the midst of it.'* I did just that. I looked up the symptoms in Louise Hay's bestselling book of psycho-emotional symptoms, *You Can Heal Your Life*. A sore throat and laryngitis are interpreted as unexpressed emotions, stifled creativity. A cough means look at me, as if you're barking at the world. Teeth represent indecisiveness. Kidneys represent anger, as do eye infections.

So, on my crack-up day, when I reached rock bottom, I decided to listen to the message and act on it so that my health would improve. I would ignore it no more. I looked at the messages – anger, indecisiveness, feelings of not being seen or heard, holding things in. What was this all about? I realized in a flood that it was a message about my relationship with my husband. We were going through one of our 'distant' patches that appear to be fine for him, but plunge me into a deep sense of loneliness. I needed more communication, so instead of stuffing my anger inside my body (usually demonstrated by lots of huffing and puffing and stomping around the house), I calmly talked to my husband. I need to talk more, I know it's my need, not yours, I said, but can we talk tonight? It was language I don't usually use. I'm generally too scared and it's far easier to stomp!

He wanted to run a mile, but he didn't and we had a good talk. We went out for breakfast together the next day, enjoyed a weekend away and suddenly the world was a better place. I don't need him to solve the problem for me, just to share it. It's a cliché, but it's true. For me, some shared moments with my husband, a visit to the homeopath, a talk with my coach, a talk with my friends are all huge balance-tippers (see Chapter 5) that ground me, give me perspective and help me connect with the emotional issues that are so easy to hide from. Above all, I acknowledged what it was that my body was trying to tell me. It had tipped out of balance because my mind and emotions were out of balance. I needed to address it and I did, and wham! I swung back into balance.

Anger

Anger is one of the most well documented causes of stress and illness. Studies have shown that the so-called type A personality, who is typically aggressive, ambitious, competitive and has a chronic sense of time urgency, is at significantly greater risk of a heart attack and coronary heart disease than a type B personality, who is more relaxed, has low levels of aggression, anxiety and time urgency and is not competitive. Further studies have managed to separate the different facets of the type A personality and have isolated 'hostility' as the main contributor to coronary heart disease.

Anger is the most toxic of emotions in the way it can impact our health. We all have anger inside us, but it has to be forced out. I've learned from my own experience that whenever I feel my emotions start to freeze, when the 'bottling' begins and the numbing occurs, I must acknowledge the anger or 'out' it – in other words do what the communication experts, relationship specialists and anger gurus suggest when they tell us to 'own' our anger. We must not blame anybody else for it. These are our emotions, our problems, and we must deal with them.

So now I don't point the finger – which is just as well, because often my anger appears to be directed towards ridiculous things such as the weather, losing something, the queues in a shop. When I accept that my anger is never really at those things, that it's always about me, I find myself laughing at the ridiculousness of my stomping body and my riotous ranting, and suddenly the anger has transformed into a joke that makes me smile if not laugh out loud. The toxic emotion has gone, it's out of the body, the sludge has turned into mercury, the energy rises and the body lifts inside. Laughter is heard in every cell as the body starts to become well.

Using this 'better out than in' method of acknowledging, outing and owning my anger sent me to full health almost immediately. My eye infection disappeared overnight, the sprained back healed and, most miraculously of all, the trip to the kidney specialist showed perfect health. My anger is now honest and constructive. My relationship is communicative again and my body's immune system is strengthening, radiating good health and vitality. It may have taken three and a half months of ill health for me to listen – surprising, perhaps, given that I already knew that the mind affects bodily health and that toxic emotions suppress the immune system – but I hope that my story sheds some light on why we ignore our body's messaging service even when we *know* it's trying to get through to us. We ignore it because we forget to listen, pretend it's not there or choose not to believe.

We will never be balanced emotionally if the body is ill, and if the body is ill, it is because emotionally we are out of balance. A body out of balance is a mind out of balance is a human out of balance – we mustn't kid ourselves otherwise. If we ignore the messages, the symptoms just get worse, teeth crack, backs ache, kidneys start bleeding and eyes start seeping pus. That is *not* a good place to be, so deal with the deeper issues and see your health improve and life return to balance. We *can* heal ourselves.

SUMMARY

Listen to the body when an 'ill' message comes in. Our minds and bodies are inextricably linked so this message is not reporting a simple body malfunction, it's telling us about an emotional 'mind' issue too, that we must not ignore. We need to look after our health because as long as we stuff our bodies full of sugar, caffeine, alcohol, nicotine or other drugs, depriving them of fresh air, exercise and regular breaks, we can forget any grand ideas of improving balance. Looking after our physical wellbeing is not a self-indulgent luxury but an essential part of the process of achieving balance.

Interactive session

Analyze your health habits
- List habits that are sabotaging your health – e.g. smoking, caffeine, alcohol, lack of fresh air, long working hours.
- Take a look at the illnesses you have, either at a low level or regularly.
- Ask friends, family and colleagues what they think you are susceptible to, or how they perceive your health.

One client who thought of themselves as very healthy was surprised to hear that he was seen as being consistently sick by his peers and partner.

Start healthy habits
- List some actions/hobbies/interests/treats that you could do which would uplift you emotionally and/or physically.
- Pick one new habit to work on for 21 days – e.g. replace caffeine with decaffeinated drinks or herbal teas, and make a note of the improvements to your health.
- Address any toxic emotions, get them out of your body, seek professional support, if necessary, from a stress counsellor, wellbeing coach or psychotherapist.

Rituals

- Divide your days into 90-minute chunks and don't work beyond that in one sitting, even if you only break for five minutes. Notice the improvement in your productivity.
- Keep a health diary. We often forget the occasions when we are feeling under par because we ignore them.
- Keep a caffeine, alcohol, nicotine diary and note how much you are having of each. Cut the amount by 10 per cent each week.
- Start to notice, read, hear inspirational stories or scientific proof – whichever means more to you – about mind/body links.

HOW . . .

to coach yourself to the work–life balance you want

— 7-day action plan

9

Coach Yourself to a Balanced Life – a 7-day Action Plan

Have you read the book and not done any of the exercises, or have you done them all and are hungry for more? Maybe, if you're the sort of person who likes practical elements, you've jumped straight to this chapter. However you've arrived here is fine. This chapter offers a mini-coaching programme for you to work through alone or with a friend or coach. It is a collection of my favourite exercises, ones that I regularly use with my clients and indeed on myself to achieve better balance in life. It is an easy programme, but it delivers stunning results. It will get you back into the driving seat.

There are seven exercises to be followed over a seven-day period. Most people find that spending a focused week with an exercise each day makes it easier to get these new principles and tools clear in their mind, but once you've grasped them and integrated them into your life, you should aim to be using them regularly. Follow the programme over a longer period if you prefer – after all, their key purpose is to help you exercise choice in your life, so how you complete these exercises should be up to you!

The journey to work–life balance is a fascinating and life-long one full of richness and discovery. Enjoy it for the very fact that it's a journey as well as a destination. See it a bit like the *Orient Express* train, a desirable journey, an exciting adventure, a luxurious experience in itself that also happens to take us to a place which, when we arrive, we can only marvel at and think: *'I've arrived in heaven.'*

Every journey requires some prerequisites in order to survive and enjoy the journey – we need food, drink and clothes. As I outlined in Chapters 6–8, I see the prerequisites on the journey to work–life balance as self-awareness, listening to our intuition and looking after our health. I have devoted a chapter to each of these, but there are numerous other requirements that will enhance our journey, the equivalents of maps, phrase books and the like. They're not essential, but they will make a difference and enable us to reach another level of interaction with our journey and destination and it is these that I have encapsulated in the exercises dotted throughout the book. Here, however, I have brought together my favourite ones. They are my favourites because they are the real life-enhancers. Think of them as keys that will help you get the best out of both the journey towards a balanced life and finally reaching your destination. I can assure you, from first-hand experience, that it is liberating, challenging, exhilarating and hugely rewarding. Think *Orient Express*!

Balancing this book

Through the process of writing this book, I have found greater balance in my life, yet I have pushed myself to the limits of my Personal Band of Balance. I have forgotten

Fathers' Day for the first year ever, forgotten to go to a leaving party for a friend who is emigrating, behaved in slightly mad and distracted ways and mislaid many things. At times, I have felt I was completely losing touch with reality, and so I have felt strangely out of balance. But, like those Weebles toys from the 1970s, I have experienced this sense of pushing the boundaries of balance in a *'Weebles-wobble-but-they-don't-fall-down'* sort of way! I have been wobbling wildly from side to side, but my wobbling has always been underpinned by a fundamental sense of choice – and thus balance.

That underlying sense of choice has made the difference, I believe, between falling out of balance and staying within my PBB – albeit only just at times! I am growing and developing and that's what the balancing act is about. It's about balancing our lives in order to achieve our full potential. Balance creates a dynamic growth opportunity. So, with my wobbling and forgetfulness have come learning, inspiration, creativity and fulfilment. Wobble, reflect, wobble, enjoy, wobble, ouch, wobble at a steady pace.

Work is at the heart of our lives for many of us and we need to honour that, so the answer is not necessarily to shy away from work or to work less. The answer is to work differently, more purposefully, to work more from our hearts, with intuition, authenticity and conscious choice. A better work–life balance heralds a more *productive* life, not a lazier one. We are not looking to shirk hard work, but aiming for a fulfilled and balanced life at work, for that is essential if we are to enjoy the other aspects of our life. To that end, therefore, we need to learn more effective ways of working that will give us the choices we want and make us feel in control. These exercises help us do that.

First of all, let me share with you some of the secrets of the coach's toolkit. I have three 'pattern-breakers' which always help focus and create a fresh and helpful perspective on any issue you are facing. Use these daily and you will notice a dramatic improvement in your resourcefulness and sense of being in control.

Pattern-breakers

We all develop patterns of behaviour that don't do us many favours but that are very tough to break. It often takes outside help to break this cycle of behaviour and this exercise is designed to do just that. When you feel yourself going out of balance, take five or ten minutes out to ask yourself these three questions. They can literally make all the difference.

- What am *I* doing that is contributing to this feeling?
- What do I *want* to happen, what is my desired outcome?
- What opportunities and options do I have to achieve that outcome? Generate as many ideas as possible.

These three questions will break the self-pitying pattern of behaviour that causes us to feel powerless or out of control. They work in the following way:

- *What am I doing that is contributing to this feeling?*

Once you have accepted that *you* are having an impact on your situation, you are taking personal responsibility. In that moment you internalize your locus of control and you give yourself choices. If it's all somebody else's fault, you can do very little to alleviate the situation.

- *What do I **want** to happen, what is my desired outcome?*

This is the simplest and most effective tool in the coaching repertoire. Focus on your desired outcome. Focus on what you actually want to happen. What do you want in your life? Most people spend so much time going through all that is problematic or challenging that they never think to ask themselves what they actually want. This is the first question any coach will ask you, for, without a desired outcome, it is impossible to take steps towards it, because you won't know where you are heading. So, if you're going to coach yourself, ask yourself that question as many times a day as you can. What do I want from this meeting? What do I want from this day? What do I want from this life of mine?

- *What opportunities and options do I have to achieve that outcome? Generate as many ideas as possible.*

This is a brilliant perspective-giver. It shows, in a matter of minutes, how many options are open to us. It focuses us on choices and gets us away from the tunnel vision of believing that there is only one way through the problem, or in many cases, no way through.

When you've asked yourself and answered these three questions, you are ready to assess the best way forward and start taking action. Coaching is about momentum, so action is vital. Pontificating is not enough. Turn your chosen options into action, and do it quickly. You're one step closer to where you want to be. In short, these three pattern-breakers are some of the most regularly used tools in a coach's toolkit. So get them out daily. I use these techniques throughout the day. I don't just reserve them for when things are going badly, although they are a great comfort and always offer a break-through. I also use them when I want to enhance my life. And I use them with clients continually, to help focus, to help see choices. If there is a single-minded message I have about balance it is the one of choice. I am extremely opti-mistic about the ability of us all to regain balance. I know when I work with people, sharing these coaching techniques and encouraging them to focus on their band of balance, success follows. It is easy. It is achievable. All it requires is a little focus, which reading this book will give you.

I would urge everyone to seek a coach, whether it be in the guise of a friend, a journal, a self-help book or a professional coach. We all benefit from someone taking the time to ask us important questions which force us to confront ourselves. For within us we have all the answers we need to resolve our balance issues. It is just that we have been too busy to look.

I know I would not have achieved my own work–life balance without the help of my coach, and balance is a topic I rejoice in having at the top of my own coaching agenda. The more I am balanced, the more I can grow. My creativity, my self-esteem, my self-knowledge have all increased, but, for me, perhaps the most important part of all is that my relation-ship with myself, my children and my friends and family is more intimate and closer than I could have imagined. I could not have achieved that by living my life at breakneck speed. I had no time for myself, let alone anyone else. I live, I work, I feel balanced. So use this chapter to act as your balance coach. Take the time to absorb yourself in the exercises, you will reap the benefits. From balance comes growth.

Exercise 1

Visualize your ideal work–life balance

Visualization has been proven to enhance the likelihood of an event occurring. It is used to improve health, mend and heal injuries, give pain relief to cancer patients. Athletes use it to increase their chances of winning a race. Many who believe that time is quantum, not linear, and that perception is reality, claim that by visualizing something you can make it real. Visualization is a powerful tool to get the results you want in your life. Here's how you can use visualization in your journey to balance:

- Close your eyes and imagine what your life would look like if you had your desired work–life balance. Notice how you look, sound and feel. Imagine being inside your body noticing your relationships with people and events. Notice the sensations in your body, your physiology and body posture and breathing. Imagine what others would notice about you that would be different. How would they feel about you? Imagine how you'd start the day, see the environments you'd be in, hear the conversations with your loved ones and your colleagues and clients. Feel the sense of serene and comfortable equipoise.
- Now capture as much of this as you can on paper. Record it. The more detail, the better.
- Now write down one small step you can take towards the desired picture that would make a difference. It

might be to wake up 10 minutes earlier so you're not so rushed in the mornings, it might be to take a proper lunchbreak, or to delegate more.

Success story

When I asked Lucy to visualize her perfect work–life balance, she was astounded because she found herself seeing two conflicting images. One was a *'steely, shiny, energetic, dynamic businesswoman who was getting a lot done, both at home and work'*, the other was a *'blue-eyed, silver, velvety woman, playing in the sunshine laughing with her children in an idyllic setting'*. She was shocked by her response to the images because she felt they were so diametrically opposed to each other. She felt that she *ought* to be the velvety woman, because that one felt like the better mother, but it didn't feel right for her. She wept with the shock but then moved on to visualize an integration of the two, where she was able to be the steely, shiny, dynamic woman *and* a velvety, soft, idyllic mother. She could be both.

We spent a long while visualizing an integration of the two. Picturing in her mind's eye the integration rather than the separation of these images helped Lucy to appreciate that there may be opportunities to work in a different way that allowed her more of what she truly wanted. She wanted the steely dynamism, and to be a soft, velvety mother as well. She started to visualize a life that could give her both, a job with a shorter commute (she was then spending up to three hours a day in the car). She visualized a job with high status and pay but with more time with her children.

Miraculous though it may seem, within a month, Lucy was offered a job that increased her pay by 50 per cent, reduced her commute to 20 minutes and was based around the corner from her children's school. She would be paid more, she would be dynamic and steely in a new high-powered role, yet be able to spend more time with her children to the extent that she'd be able to take them to school each day. Needless to say, she accepted! Co-incidence? Maybe, but it's got to be worth a try.

Exercise 2

Making the most of energy

Working with rather than against our natural energy rhythms throughout the day can enhance our performance significantly. We know instinctively that some of us are larks and some of us owls. Struggling to have a high performance at your low energy slump times goes against the flow. Make it easy on yourself. Draw an energy chart and note when you have your peaks and troughs throughout the day.

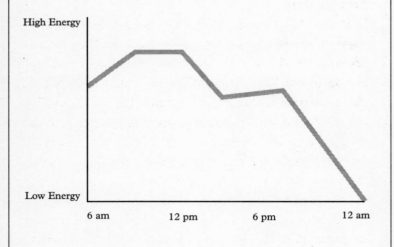

Energy chart

- Plot your energy pattern across the day.
- Note when your high points and slumps occur. People often find such charts very gratifying as they have often not thought about the impact of energy levels on their daily routine.
- Organize your life/diary to maximize your energy highs and lows – e.g. do an energizing task during your slump periods and do your most productive work in your high energy slots.
- Arrange to take a walk – outside if possible or round the office if not – around the time of your lowest point. You won't get anything done in that time sitting at your desk.

Success story

June found that she had very high energy in the morning, a slump around lunch and again for a couple of hours from about 4 o'clock, then another surge of energy around 6 pm. What she discovered was that she would often promise to be home at a time that meant leaving the office at 6-ish, but would become so engaged and caught up in her surge of energy after an afternoon of lassitude and lethargy that she would lose track of time, leave the office late, and end up feeling guilty she had broken her promise again. Once she was home she would feel tired and distracted, thereby impacting negatively on her family life. Once she realized what her energy rhythms were, she used her morning high energy to work on all the meaty projects, used her slump time to do tasks that were naturally energizing to her (in her case critiquing documents or papers and doing spread-sheet analysis) and left the office just prior to her after-noon surge of energy so that her family were able to be on the receiving end of that high. Twice a week she pre-planned staying at the office later to take advan-tage of it at work but, because it was pre-planned, both her family and she felt in control and knew it was a choice. The end result was a happy June, a happy family, and a self-confessed 'excellent' work–life balance.

Exercise 3

Locus of control

People who have an internal locus of control – i.e. perceive that they have control over their lives – are empirically proven to be more successful, confident and healthier, plus they have a better sense of wellbeing than those who have an external locus of control or who perceive that they have no control over their lives, that things just happen to them. This exercise is designed to bring your locus of control right inside.

- Think about a situation that you feel frustrated about, where you perceive you have little or no power over things.
- Now list all the things that you are doing or *not* doing that may be contributing to this.
- Once you have your list, think of alternative ways to handle some or all of the issues on the list.

Success story

A senior management team was recently subject to a takeover by a large corporation. The resulting clash of cultures resulted in redundancies and a demotivated group of managers who felt helpless, disempowered, unable to motivate their own teams, anxious, out of control and depressed. I discussed the concept of locus of control with this group and they realized that they had let their locus of control become external, so that things were happening *to* them. In their minds they felt they had no choice, no control over what would happen next. *'If we only knew what their strategy was, or their vision, we could help more'*, they lamented. These managers, like all of us, wanted meaning to their work and to be able to contribute.

After identifying that their locus of control was external, we then worked on internalizing it. They listed all the things they were or weren't doing that were contributing to the situation.

Were doing
- Moaning.
- Expecting the new CEO to mind-read.
- Demotivating themselves and their teams.
- Focusing on all the bad things.
- Refusing to adopt different methods of working.

Weren't doing
- Asking clarifying questions.
- Asking for the strategy or vision to be explained.
- Being proactive.
- Talking among themselves positively.
- Finding out what their teams needed to know.

By identifying these points, they internalized the locus of control. Acknowledging that *'it isn't them, it's us – it's how we're dealing with it that's causing us to feel this way'* enabled them to take control of the situation. Suddenly, through this shift to personal responsibility and the acceptance that they were contributing to their own misery, they felt empowered.

They asked the CEO, who was based in the USA, to come and outline his vision. They conducted a questionnaire to elicit all anxieties from their employees, to ensure that they or the CEO could address the concerns. They realized the impact of their mood and focus on their teams, so they worked as a group to be more proactive and positive. Depression and demotivation were soon replaced with energy and focus. The locus of control had been internalized.

Exercise 4

Looking back to go forward

So busy are we moving on to the next stage in our lives that we often forget to look back and learn valuable lessons from our past. But when we do take the time to look back with the benefit of hindsight we see things with a fresh perspective that enables us to look for trends and patterns that can feed and inspire our future. I encourage you to use a creative right-brain technique with the following exercise so you don't over-analyze and paralyze your thought.

- Using the metaphor of a river, draw a 'river of change' which represents the last ten years of your life. Draw the river however you like, with whatever flow you like, and include anything or any person that you feel needs to be there. Some people draw rapids, waterfalls, tributaries, bridges, people, rafts – it's your choice.
- Draw it quickly – don't try and be logical (yet).
- Capture themes. Get a friend or coach to ask you questions if you prefer to do it with someone. For example, you might notice where the river gets wider or narrower, where it flows quickly or slowly and what that represents in your life.
- Notice what constitutes the good times.
- Now get logical. What lessons can you learn from your picture?

Success story

Marie did this exercise, looking back over the last three years. She was surprised with the overall pattern of her river, which widened over time, representing her growth and development, so she received a very positive message from the exercise about how far she'd come. She then noticed that the happiest times were not periods of still waters, despite the fact that this is what she claimed she was after, still waters representing for Marie quiet times at work. The period that had given her greatest pleasure was when she was actually busy and challenged at work, but not out of control. From this she developed a work strategy that related to her Personal Band of Balance – i.e. if she found herself too busy, she cut back immediately, if she found herself in a quiet period, she sought out some new projects. This promoted a sense of wellbeing, happiness and balance for Marie.

Exercise 5

Life currencies

Money is just one currency in our lives. In order to understand what the other ones are in your life, you have to imagine a kind of trade-off. It's hard but it focuses the mind! The following exercise is most effective if done with coach or friend, but it can easily be done alone too.

- List all the things that are important as 'currencies' in your life. Try to keep to between five and seven. They might include time, health, children, home, clothes, learning.
- Write each one on a different piece of paper.
- Hold one in one hand and choose another.
- Ask if you *had* to choose just one of the two 'currencies', which it would be?
- Force yourself to make a clear choice. Faced with a choice between health and money, for example, don't avoid the question by answering *'Well, as long as I had enough money to live on, I'd choose health.'*
- Make a note of every choice and weigh all of them against each other in every combination so that you end up with a hierarchy of your life currencies.
- Notice the order. It is always surprising!
- Once you know your hierarchy of currencies think about whether you are living your life to make the most of the most important currencies in your life. So, if time is more important to you than money,

devise strategies that give you more time, even if it is less money. If health is more important than a nice house, start looking at ways to nurture your health rather than focusing on moving up the property ladder.

Success story

Lee-anne did this exercise and found that a beautiful home was her top currency (she had grown up in a pub, with an alcoholic father, who died when she was a teenager). A beautiful home was a sanctuary to her. She decided she wanted to change jobs but that the most important thing was her home. She focused on earning just enough to keep her home. She was willing for her salary to be cut by two-thirds if that meant she could work from home. Lee-anne had her life currencies sorted. Home was more important than money. A beautiful home nurtured her health, wellbeing and creativity.

Exercise 6

Drawing on the hidden answers

Drawing is a 'right-brain' activity. It is creative, intuitive and makes connections in our brain synapses that are completely different to those we make when we write or speak. If you want to find a creative solution to a problem, draw or use images. This is my personal favourite as an exercise and I always use it when I feel low, anxious, confused or stressed. I just let my pen glide across the page, not knowing what will come up, but the answer is always there and often a real surprise. The exercise taps into the great creativity of our unconscious minds and will help you access yours.

- Draw your situation at work, as it is now.
- Draw your ideal situation at work.
- Now draw your life as it is now, including work.
- Draw your life as you want it to be.
- Note the themes, capture the issues, and discuss them with a partner, friend, colleague or coach. You will have tapped into an underlying issue.

Success story

Leo felt he was in a very difficult relationship with his CEO. He was gunning to be promoted but always felt undermined by him. When I asked him to draw pictures of his current situation and his ideal situation, he drew just one picture, which showed two groups; the first consisted of the CEO with lots of other people, the second group consisted of just one person, which depicted him outside this group. His ideal picture was that he was *within* the other group. He realized in that moment that the problem wasn't to do with his relationship with the CEO, but about his sense of exclusion from his peers. Leo felt left out. He therefore shifted his focus to being more sociable and inclusive with his colleagues instead of being rather standoffish and waiting for them to include him in their activities. His sense of understanding exactly what the issue was and his immediate sense of being proactive in dealing with the situation unleashed a great sense of purpose and confidence within him. Three months later he was promoted.

Exercise 7

Slowing down

It's scary to slow down. We hanker after a more leisurely pace yet we hate it. There is a tension, for in slowing down we have to face the possibilities that we all fear on some level – what if we get bored or don't like what we find? If we keep busy we can avoid confronting this, but, in fact, slowing down is the biggest gift we can give ourselves, our friends and families and our organizations. By slowing down we speed up our effectiveness and live life rather than life living us. This exercise helps slow you down, filling your life with riches you couldn't imagine. Joy and inner peace rarely enter a crammed schedule.

- Drop your caffeine intake (tea, coffee, chocolate, cola, etc) for one week. At the same time, drop one meeting a day. Notice the difference as you calm down.
- Use the saved time to be 'intentional' about the next part of the day. Take 5–10 minutes just to focus on what you want to achieve, receive, feel by the end of the day.
- Keep notes on your energy levels and productivity this week.

Success story

Jane spent the first two days still spinning, the drop in caffeine gave her a headache and she felt no energy increase. She filled her 'spare' time with crazy things such as moving the furniture in her office, cleaning things out. Then, on the third day, she noticed a decided shift, she felt calmer and lighter. She felt a surge of energy as a result of releasing herself from meetings, which she realized weren't vital, just time consuming.

She started to use her extra time to write down her intentions. She focused on three months hence. As a CEO she found she had suddenly given herself strategy-thinking time, which allowed her to lift herself out of a day-to-day reactive stance and gave her valuable thinking time. She was so encouraged that she started to diarize this thinking time first thing in the morning, and to keep note of the initiatives that came out of the session. Her newly calm demeanour also gave her a less frenetic appearance, which people commented on positively, saying she looked and seemed more in control. That's not surprising, because she was.

One year on, and with a string of significant business and personal successes under her belt, Jane told me what her biggest accomplishment in the previous year had been. I'd expected an answer about growth in profit or winning new business, but she instantly said: *'That's easy – it was slowing down. It's that one achievement that led to all the others. I'm not just a better CEO, I'm a better friend, wife and mother, and I'm healthier.'*

Conclusion

You can do it. You can have more balance. We all can. We deserve a life that is fully lived not half-lived. It's time to wake up, take that choice and live life the way we want to, balancing the fulfilment and stimulation of meaningful work and meaningful achievements in our home life with authentic relationships in both our work and our home life.

It saddens me to end this book, such has been the joy and experience and learning in the search to solve the mystery of work–life balance. I've loved it, but it will only really achieve its goal if it helps people get their lives back on track. If it helps people live a life that makes sense to them, where they can connect again with the world around them, then my goal will be achieved.

So I leave it with you, for, as you well know by now . . . it's your choice. Exercise it well.

Fiona would love to hear feedback from you, so please do write to her:

Fiona Parashar
c/o Simon & Schuster UK Ltd,
Africa House, 64-78 Kingsway,
London WC2B 6AH

She is also available for workshops, coaching and speaking. For a full range of services, take a look at her website:
www.leadershipcoaching.co.uk